SIMPLIFY Y

NAOMI SAUNDERS is a 'clu
simplification is the cure for str _002 she founded
Clearly Organised, a de-cluttering consultancy, advising
individuals and businesses on reducing and reorganizing
to make space for growth and change. She writes and
broadcasts regularly about stress and clutter and how to
free ourselves from both. Naomi lives with her husband
and two children in Reading.

Overcoming Common Problems Series

Selected titles

A full list of titles is available from Sheldon Press,
36 Causton Street, London SW1P 4ST and on our website at
www.sheldonpress.co.uk

Overcoming Common Problems

Simplify Your Life

Downsize and De-stress

Naomi Saunders

sheldon**PRESS**

First published in Great Britain in 2006

Sheldon Press
36 Causton Street
London SW1P 4ST

Copyright © Naomi Saunders 2006

British Library Cataloguing-in-Publication Data

A catalogue record for this book is available from the British Library

ISBN-13: 978–0–85969–972–3
ISBN-10: 0–85969–972–2

1 3 5 7 9 10 8 6 4 2

Typeset by Deltatype Limited, Birkenhead, Merseyside
Printed in Great Britain by Ashford Colour Press

Contents

In memory of my cousin Richard Axon
1963–2006

Acknowledgements

With love and thanks to my children Roberta and Huw, who survived with minimal parenting while I wrote this book, and to Gareth, who listened patiently to all my ideas and didn't burst my bubble. My thanks also go to Roisin McAuley, for all her encouragement and wise words, Ali Phillpotts, my de-clutter companion and steadfast friend, and Vivienne Loren, without whom I would never have got started.

Finally, I owe a huge debt of gratitude to all my clients who so freely allowed me into the darkest and most cluttered corners of their homes and lives.

Introduction

There seems to be an undercurrent of panic to Western society at the moment. No one lives a simple life any more. Everyone rushes about, multi-tasking like mad, trying to squeeze too many things into too short a time. You can have drive thru' meals, quick-drying nail polish, power naps, read abridged books, have someone else do your shopping, text instead of speak. Too many things are disposable. We add to landfill on a daily basis as we throw old things out in favour of new. We have become slaves to immediate gratification, and never mind about the future.

Many of the people that I visit in the course of my work as a 'clutter doctor' have reached a critical point in their lives, when they feel totally overwhelmed by their possessions and trapped by all their commitments. They may be working long hours, their stress levels are high, and they are often depressed and not coping well with daily tasks. They are often time-impoverished, their lives are over-complicated, and they feel they are just running to stand still.

Workers in the UK still work the longest hours in Europe, with the average working week being 39.6 hours (New Earnings Survey, April 2002). Although some employers have started to offer family-friendly practices, such as working more hours earlier in the week so that you can finish early on Fridays, it's still tough trying to fit everything in if you're working and bringing up a family. Days are a blur of work, mealtimes, television, bed . . . and then it starts all over again. You are probably irritable, humourless and stressed.

Stress is the greatest cause of absence from work – it lowers your immune system so you fall prey to any virus that's going around. You drink, eat and smoke more just to help you cope with the stress, and exercise less because you don't have time. Are you working to live or living to work? We spend increasing amounts of time working ever harder to earn more money simply to buy back more time.

Many people are working hard to fund a lifestyle that they can't really afford. They are like poor old Sisyphus, who was condemned by the Greek gods to a lifetime of pointless labour, continuously rolling a rock up to the top of a mountain, only for it to fall all the way back down again upon reaching the crest. Every time he thought he had made it, the task began all over again. Sounds familiar?

How many of us continue to live comfortably up to our means, but then, just as we get on an even keel, decide that it's time to take on more? We increase our financial commitments by taking on a bigger mortgage. We own a bigger house and fill it with yet more things. We apply for more credit and have to take on more work to fund it. We find ourselves with a bit of spare time and squeeze in another commitment. Although we might *talk* about the attractions of a simpler life, we still find ourselves locked into the same old trap, with no time and not enough money. Why are we so bad at recognizing our own comfort zones?

There is far more to life than working all hours to earn enough money to buy a big house to fill with possessions. You may spend your whole life always striving for more and still never be satisfied – what a waste! The only certainty facing any of us is that one day we will die, and then what will happen to all those precious things that we spent our lives acquiring, finding space for and worrying about? Someone else will inherit them and have to worry about them instead of us. That person may even just throw them away!

In my work, I see the benefits of a simpler life repeatedly. People often contact me after they have reduced their possessions and simplified their lives, telling me they feel liberated, lighter, and able to think more clearly. Whether you want to be more in control of your time, your money, or your space, this book will help you. It will show you how to keep your immediate environment manageable, how not to waste time on things that don't matter, and how to expend your energy on the people and activities that are of true value to you. I can guarantee that if you follow these simple directions towards a simpler life, you really will lose a major part of your stress, and gain a wonderful new sense of emotional freedom.

Clearing away your physical and mental clutter can act as a catalyst for change in all areas of your life. It can have a hugely positive effect on your mental state, helping to clear your mind, which in turn helps you to see your way forward. You will be able to plan ahead and make more changes so that you are able to enjoy a life that is not only deeply satisfying, but that really expresses you. If you make space in your life, change will always follow.

INTRODUCTION

Go confidently in the direction of your dreams! Live the life you've imagined. As you simplify your life, the laws of the universe will be simpler.

Henry David Thoreau, 1817–62

1
Simplicity and its benefits

Have you ever wished that life were less complicated? Are you constantly struggling to have enough time, money and space? Are you envious of those who have a simpler lifestyle?

I believe that one of the key things that make our lives complicated and stressful is ownership of too much stuff. During my years as a 'clutter doctor' I have seen repeatedly how people are trapped by their possessions, stressed out by the very things they have worked so hard to acquire. Seeing inside so many homes, I have discovered that people seem to have a love/hate relationship with what they own; they attach too much importance to it, don't feel able to get rid of it, but then feel bogged down by it. I often receive e-mails and phone calls from people telling me that they can't stand living with their possessions any more and that they want to get rid of everything and start again with empty rooms. People spend half their lives acquiring things and the rest of the time trying to get rid of them. How crazy is that?

It's a normal human impulse to want to acquire things and, for women particularly, collecting and home-making are instinctive. However, it's good to keep a perspective on ownership and learn to say no to your acquisitive impulse sometimes. Take a good look at your life. Does it have to be so complicated? Could you live it more simply and slowly if you really tried? Could you make changes that would decrease your spending and stress, and increase your time? All these are possible.

The trend towards simplicity

Over the last few years there has been an increasing trend towards a simpler life. In the USA, the 'simple living' or 'voluntary simplicity' movement, which began in the early 1980s, has taken off, as people aim to free themselves from stress and create more balance in their lives. About 5–7 per cent of adults in the USA are pursuing some form of voluntary simplicity, according to Gerald Celente, director of the Trends Research Institute in New York. Dozens of books, magazines, websites and grassroots 'simplicity circles' have sprung up for those interested in scaling back. (See Useful addresses at the back of this book.)

Consumerism has reached a peak. I am certain that the pendulum has swung as far as it can go in one direction and we are on the brink of a massive swing back to simplicity. A BBC documentary, where psychologists looked into the psychology of shopping and consumerism, revealed that – surprise, surprise – consumerism can increase stress.

People in the UK are disenchanted with consumerism, according to a survey by the Women's Environmental Network, and events where people can swap household goods and unwanted gifts are enjoying a boom.

A whole raft of lifestyle programmes on television, as well as an abundance of books and magazines, show us how to eat properly, get fitter, dress better, manage our money, look after our children and, of course, clear our clutter! The growing trend for a return to old-fashioned family values, better-behaved children, the resurgence of the housewife as a respected profession, and a desire for increased spiritual awareness cannot be ignored.

In 2004, the Neuropsychiatric Institute at the University of California in Los Angeles (UCLA) (now the Semel Institute of Neuroscience and Human Behavior) held a conference called 'Mental Health and Simple Living: Countering the *Compulsion to Consume*', where complexity was identified as a key factor in a 'toxic' culture where we need voluntary simplicity as a 'therapeutic tool'. According to Peter Whybrow, MD, Director of UCLA's Neuropsychiatric Institute, and author of *American Mania: When More Is Not Enough*:

> We have created for ourselves an environment which is extraordinarily complex and very affluent in terms of choice. That is, I believe, beginning to create a situation where we are pushing the limits of human physiology. Some people collapse a little earlier than others as this push occurs, but in the long run this is not a story about people who have mental illness, this is a story about all of us.

The desire for simplicity also manifests itself in home design. After the fussy opulence of the 1980s, the stripped pine and chintz of the

1990s and the minimalism of the millennium years, designers have now turned to nostalgic simplicity. Copies of Grandma's storage tins abound in kitchenware departments, simple cotton floral prints are 'in', sheets and blankets are back on our beds, home-baking and knitting have enjoyed a renaissance, and it's OK to be a full-time mum again!

Across the world, 'slow movements' are springing up in response to the 'fast' epidemic. In Italy, the Slow Food movement started in 1986, as a protest against plans for a McDonald's restaurant that was to be built at the Spanish Steps in Rome. The Slow Food manifesto states, 'We are enslaved by speed and have all succumbed to the same insidious virus: Fast Life, which disrupts our habits, pervades the privacy of our homes and forces us to eat Fast Foods.'

My own story

Around the same time that I started my business, my husband, Gareth, and I decided to try to move up the property ladder, hoping to leave the house we had lived in for 12 years and move into a large Victorian detached villa – the house of my dreams. It meant a large mortgage repayment for us every month and I knew my husband was secretly worried about it. Although it was the house of *my* dreams, I knew that it wasn't the house that Gareth would have chosen. Even so, I became completely focused on it and wanted it above all else. I spent hours at our local records office, researching its history and I knew exactly who had lived there since it had been built. In my imagination I furnished all the rooms and even bought curtains for some of the windows.

The months dragged on and I drove past the house every day, impatient for it to be ours. However, on the day of exchange, the buyer at the beginning of our purchasing chain decided to pull out and the sale collapsed, like the proverbial house of cards.

After seven stressful months of highs and lows, the house I had mentally moved into was back on the market and immediately snapped up by another purchaser. I was devastated and felt I had suffered a major loss. I knew I had been foolish to want it so much and I looked even more foolish now I didn't have it. My poor husband, thoroughly worn out by the emotional rollercoaster of the previous six months, vowed we would never again be caught up in a property chain and decided that we should move into rented accommodation so we could be cash buyers when we looked for another house.

Within a few months we had moved out to a small bungalow in the countryside. We had to do some major downsizing to fit into a smaller space, and much of our furniture and possessions went into temporary storage in the garage.

What began as a temporary measure for us became a way of life. We discovered a great freedom in having less stuff, and after a while couldn't even remember what was in the garage, let alone miss having it in the house! I realized how few things we really needed and began to look at our possessions with new eyes. Did I really *like* all of these objects that I had been hanging on to for so many years? Were they truly useful items in my life and did I anticipate using them again? The more I thought about things the less I wanted them.

At the same time, I was seeing clients every week who were completely bogged down by their possessions and whose finances were in a mess because of bad spending habits and the desire to own too much stuff. Many of them were depressed and struggling to make ends meet – all of them were dissatisfied with their lives. It seemed to me that the more things people had, the less happy they were. The more possessions they owned, the more stuff they were responsible for. They had to think about it, decide what to do with it, move it around from place to place, and worry about how to get rid of it. They had to buy bigger and better homes to accommodate their growing piles of possessions and then wanted to update all those possessions to go with their new home. They were caught in a vicious circle of earning and acquiring – and stress.

Gradually I came to understand that I didn't want this for myself, or my family. I saw that a big house full of stuff doesn't necessarily make you happy, and simplicity suddenly became a much more attractive option. We had fewer possessions and a smaller house – so what? We also had no mortgage, no buildings maintenance and no financial worries. We were able to rent a home in a beautiful village where we could never afford to buy, and our children enjoyed the luxury of being able to walk to school and live near all their friends. The community reached out and welcomed us and we thrived on village life.

Free from the endless round of school runs and home improvements, I was able to focus entirely on caring for my family and growing my business, and even found some time to concentrate on hobbies and interests I had abandoned years ago. My husband, secretly much relieved that the 'dream home' had fallen through, was able to spend time updating his skills and redirecting his career, as well as fulfilling some of his personal ambitions. Together we spent time looking at our finances and planning for the future.

Without the distraction of keeping up with the Jones's, I was able to spend more time on the things that mattered most: loving my family, being a better friend, knowing myself more, and understanding what I really wanted to do.

I am telling you this not because I am putting my life on a pedestal, but because I am a normal individual who, like most others, wants a nice home and nice things around me, but who feels there must be more to life than always earning more in order to buy more. I would still like a nice home, but not at the expense of a happy family life and the health of my husband. A simpler life is more attractive in many ways.

Benefits of simplicity

Because of the nature of my work, I know that simplicity works for many people, giving them a wonderful new sense of freedom and clarity, with a much more defined direction in life.

Being disorganized is an incredibly stressful state to live in and can impact seriously on your total well-being. Living day to day in chaos will eventually affect your health as you struggle to maintain everything and become increasingly despondent. If every room and passageway in your house is clogged up with stuff, it means that there is no clear flow of energy around your home. You will probably feel sluggish and tired, totally lacking in motivation and unable to make any progress with anything. Stagnant energy and piles of clutter impact not only on your physical space, but also on your mental well-being. Too much clutter can also:

- Make you feel confused and disorganized.
- Affect your breathing, especially if you're asthmatic.
- Stop you sleeping well.
- Make you depressed.
- Impact on your relationships.

- Prevent you from making progress in all areas of your life.
- Waste your time.
- Use up precious space.

Simplifying your life is a major factor in reducing stress and improving your energy levels. Some medical research shows that a simpler life may have health benefits, helping with tension-related reactions such as insomnia, anxiety, neck and shoulder pain, and chronic fatigue.

In a study published in the journal *Social Science & Medicine*, researchers from Ohio State University and the University of Alabama found that people with a high ratio of credit card debt to income were in worse physical health than those with less debt.

Another study by the University of Rochester Medical Center looked at the way women's memory appears to decline in middle life; and the results suggest that the issue is not really impaired memory, but instead is due to stress, which prevents women taking in the information in the first place. Put simply, women are often too stretched to take in or 'encode' new information; when people spread their attention too thinly, it's difficult to listen properly to new information.

Recognizing stress

You probably know whether you're under stress or not, but some common signs of too much stress include:

- Increased irritability.
- Heightened sensitivity to criticism.
- Signs of tension, such as nail-biting.
- Difficulty in getting to sleep and early morning waking.
- Increased use of alcohol or cigarettes.
- Indigestion.
- Loss of concentration.

While stress alone does not cause specific illnesses, it can result in several short-term stress-related effects such as tiredness, headaches, digestive problems and muscle tension, as well as psychological problems such as disturbed sleep, low self-esteem, mood swings, anxiety and poor concentration. Long term, sustained stress can increase our chances of a range of illnesses, such as heart problems, infections and diabetes, depending on our individual genetic inheritance, and on our lifestyle. Because higher amounts of the stress hormone cortisol are generated, our bodies may respond in various ways – with raised blood pressure, an altered balance of the immune system, and increased blood glucose levels. Research at Queen Charlotte's and Chelsea Hospital in London has shown that stress and anxiety may even cause women to give birth to smaller babies.

To sum up, some of the benefits of a simpler life might be:

- Less stress.
- Better health.
- More time to spend how you wish.
- Less wastage.
- More money saved.
- More environmentally friendly.
- Less consumer-driven.
- More personal peace and contentment.
- More enjoyment of special things.

The simplicity of the Amish communities

For the Amish communities of Pennsylvania in the USA, simplicity is a chosen way of life. There is a general curiosity about the way they live – the Harrison Ford film *Witness* romanticized the simplicity, while 'Shaker style' furniture and household items have found appeal in homes throughout the world. Many people are charmed and intrigued by this simple way of living, but could we really manage it ourselves?

Outsiders rarely, if ever, enter the Amish community; those not born into it often find the lifestyle too austere and hard to understand. Community, family and humility are the most important things for the Amish people and one of their major beliefs is that they, as a community, should remain separate and independent from the rest of the world. Any change is carefully examined before it is accepted and, even then, only embraced if it helps retain the simple lifestyle.

For example, the Amish do not use electricity as they believe that electrical wires link them to the outside world and could therefore lead to temptation and the consequent deterioration of family life. Most of us would consider it impossible to live without electricity. Computers, television, radio, household appliances – and all other things that we take for granted – are things that the Amish manage to live quite happily without. I'm not suggesting that any of us should try to take on the Amish lifestyle, but there are elements of it that we should pay attention to. The family as a central focus, the use of shared skills within the community, and making things instead of buying them, are all valuable examples that we could follow and are easily transferable to non-Amish life.

Retreats

For outsiders, the Amish lifestyle can seem over-strict and a little strange. Yet they have a deep faith. Is there a correlation between faith and simplicity? Certainly, the fewer possessions you have, the less distracted you are by worldly goods and the more you can concentrate on your beliefs and your feelings. I don't know if simplicity of surroundings indicates purity of heart or mind, but there is a growing trend for spiritual retreats where individuals feeling the 'burn-out' of a too busy life can withdraw from the noise and frenetic pace that for many people has become the norm. Simple surroundings, few distractions and the opportunity for quiet contemplation and introspection can all help to restore personal balance and perspective.

Some retreats are run along religious lines, others are secular, but all provide the opportunity for spiritual refreshment and rejuvenation. Retreat-type breaks offer stillness and silence, rare things in this noisy world, and give us the time to listen to our inner voice, which most of the time we ignore. We have become adept at shutting off our true feelings and functioning on a shallow and mechanical level. Many people are quite apprehensive about investigating their true feelings – sometimes it's easier to stay on the treadmill than get off and think about things.

So do any of us ever take time to really listen to our hearts? More and more people these days are recognizing the need to attend to their own spirituality and there is a move towards this in many areas – for example, self-help books, courses, evening classes, holidays and support groups. (See details of the Retreat Association in the Useful addresses section at the back of this book.)

Peak oil crisis

We are told that in the space of only a few more generations the world will be facing a massive oil crisis. Energy prices will rise, supplies will run low – and possibly even run out. The Association for the Study of Peak Oil (ASPO) says that the rising price of oil will affect virtually every aspect of our lives and, unless an alternative power source can be found, the way we live now will have to change radically. How will we run our cars, heat our houses, and keep using all our electrical appliances? Will the cost of food go up in line with the cost of transporting it? Will we face shortages of things because we can no longer get hold of them? Will we stop seeing members of our family because it's too expensive to travel?

With less or no petrol, families will become less mobile. This, coupled with a rising elderly population, could mean that the extended family unit and three-generation living will once again become the norm, as families choose to stay nearer to one another.

Less mobility will affect the way we work, shop, travel, run our families, go on holiday and enjoy our leisure time. Living a simpler life may become a necessity and not just a matter of choice.

We cannot continue to live only for the moment, and should start to make conscientious choices about the way we are living now, in order to pave the way to a better future for our children and subsequent generations. To make very small changes in your life might seem futile and of little consequence, but it can never be wrong to strive for a better, simpler and less wasteful way of living.

Some simple pleasures

There is value and enjoyment to be had from many simple things. They need not be expensive – they might even be free! Get out of the habit of thinking you have to spend money to enjoy yourself. Here are some ideas to start you off. You will have others, I'm sure.

- Look round an art gallery.
- Go for a walk in a beautiful place.

- Catch up with friends you haven't seen for ages.
- Read a good book.
- Have special family nights.
- If you have children, let them cook for you.
- Do more gardening – even if this means 'sprouting seeds' on the kitchen window sill.
- Listen to the radio.
- Do a jigsaw with members of the family.
- Bake a cake and invite friends over to share it.
- Join a choir.
- Visit a museum.
- If you live near the sea, walk on the beach and go shell gathering.
- Go dancing.
- Learn to knit.
- Sort out your photos.
- Write your family history.
- Do some voluntary work.
- Organize a bring and buy sale for charity.
- Go on a bike ride.
- De-clutter a drawer.
- De-clutter a whole room!
- Meditate.
- Have a laugh.
- Go trampolining.
- Help someone less fortunate than you.
- Explore your area.
- Go to a jumble sale.
- Start a patchwork quilt.
- Do something else that is creative.
- Make something you can use.
- Write a letter.

TOP TIP: Don't worry what others might think of any lifestyle changes you make – it really doesn't matter. Some people might be fearful that you will succeed where they haven't. Stop your treadmill and get off for a while – you might enjoy it!

2

Why our lives become complicated

Many of you reading this book will have chosen it because you feel your life has become too complicated and stressful, and you are attracted to the idea of downsizing and simplifying. You may not wish to 'quit the rat-race' entirely, but perhaps you'd just like to run it more slowly! If, like most people, you are trying to run a family, attend to your relationships, be successful at your job, keep everyone happy, have enough money, and stay debt-free, it may all just be too much.

However, you *can* think about reasons why your life might have become complicated – for example, why you own so much stuff, why you always need to earn more, why you never feel satisfied – and decide if there are things that you can change or areas of your life that you can simplify. This will be discussed in more detail in Chapter 3.

So why do our lives become so complicated?

Consumer pressure

This is a major force behind our over-complex lives. How is it that we have so much these days, so many material possessions and wonderful opportunities, yet we're still not satisfied? Television, newspapers and magazines constantly encourage us to want more, buy more and do more. Credit is easily obtained, and waiting until you can afford something is seen as old-fashioned and unnecessary, particularly by the younger generation. We are led to believe we *can* have it all. However, this constant 'must have it now' attitude only increases our appetite for material possessions and leaves us always wanting more. Happiness is always just one more 'thing' away.

We are being swept along by intensive marketing, making us feel inadequate or undesirable without those special items. We are being sold the perfect lifestyle, which, like the Emperor's new clothes, doesn't really exist.

The balance has been lost. For many people, their spending has spiralled out of control and they are irretrievably in debt. More stuff

11

just makes our lives increasingly complicated, debt-laden, and exhausting.

Possessions

Ownership is such a status symbol in our consumer culture, yet I have never met anyone with loads of stuff who has been made happy by it (usually quite the reverse). Obviously, it's easier to feel OK if you're not worrying about owning the basics, but it's a misconception that the more you have the happier you are. In his book *The Pursuit of Happiness*, David G. Myers argues that while we are twice as rich as we were 40 years ago, depression rates have soared. You only need to pick up a glossy magazine to read about high-profile, high-income celebrities who appear to have it all, yet suffer from depression, eating disorders, or drug- and alcohol-related illnesses.

I'm not saying that material wealth equals poverty of spirit, or that the less you have the more spiritually aware you are (although there are some religious orders who believe this), but nevertheless there are people who feel they need a certain level of ownership in order to feel complete.

Becoming the owner of too many possessions doesn't happen overnight – it's usually the end result of a long process, which, for some people, starts in early childhood. Emotional deprivation as a child can result in a person substituting material goods for love and affection in later life. More commonly, material deprivation in childhood means that an individual may be reluctant to get rid of things as an adult: the fear of not having enough always providing a stronger pull than the desire for a less cluttered life. Some of my most overloaded clients have come from very poor backgrounds, and although they are now comfortably able to afford whatever they need, they are still very cautious when it comes to getting rid of things (see the case study of Fran in Chapter 9).

What money can't buy

We often tend to overlook these:

- Love.
- Lost time.
- Good health.

- Spending time with people we care about.
- Spiritual contentment.
- Peace and quiet.
- Satisfaction of helping others.

Why we hang on to things: excuses, excuses

As a professional organizer I am privileged to see inside many houses and hear many people's stories. It's a fascinating job and I'm so lucky to do something that I really enjoy. If there's a downside, it's that I sometimes get frustrated hearing the same old excuses from people about why they have so much stuff and why they want to keep it, while at the same time saying they want to simplify their lives.

By the time clients call me they are usually pretty desperate. Yet, although people know they are cluttered, when it comes to the crunch of getting rid of things, they get cold feet and the excuses come thick and fast! If only I could convince them how much better they'll feel once their clutter has diminished and how much they will enjoy the resulting sense of space and emotional freedom.

Top ten excuses for hanging on to things (and my responses)

1 It might come in handy someday. *(It won't.)*
2 You can't get hold of these any longer. *(You probably can – just use the internet.)*
3 It was given to me. *(Doesn't mean you have to keep it.)*
4 I'm saving it to give to someone. *(But will they really want it?)*
5 It might be worth something. *(Only if you sell it.)*
6 I might slim into it. *(You won't.)*
7 It cost a lot of money. (. . . and it wastes a lot of space.)
8 It just needs mending. *(So how long has it been broken?)*
9 I'll keep it as a spare. *(You've already got several spares.)*
10 The children might like it. *(They won't.)*

'It might come in handy one day!'

I often work with older clients who were born, and grew up, during the Second World War: the wartime 'thrift' generation. They were taught to be careful and nothing was wasted. Things were used until they fell apart, at which point they were fixed by the chap down the road, or used for something else; our grandparents were the ultimate recyclers! Getting rid of something just because you 'fancied a new one' was unheard of – there was neither the choice of goods, nor the money, for such wanton extravagance. I admire the wonderful 'make do and mend' philosophy of the war years and believe we could all learn from our older generations.

My maternal grandparents, born at the end of the nineteenth century, were good working-class people, who survived two world wars, and lived a simple and loving life. They lived in the same little terraced house for all of their long married life (75 years), with furniture that they had saved up for during their engagement. The house itself cost them £450 in 1926; they bought it outright and never had a mortgage. They led an uncomplicated life, with few possessions and a strict daily routine. They didn't have an indoor loo or bathroom until the 1970s, nor a telephone until the 1980s. Every Sunday, Grandpa walked to the phone box at the end of the street and called us, otherwise they kept in touch by letter. He walked everywhere or caught the bus – he never owned a car or learned to drive – and if he couldn't get somewhere on a bus, he didn't go. Grandpa was a wonderful gardener and Grandma was the world's best knitter. They were devoted parents and grandparents and relished life's smallest pleasures. My grandfather lived until he was 102 and my grandmother until she was 99 – that's what I call a good life!

I grew up in the 1960s, a vicarage child. Money was never plentiful; the stipend for a country clergyman was woefully small in those days, but with my mother's inherent thriftiness and my father's careful budgeting, we never went short. I don't remember wishing for anything more than I had, and certainly never felt I missed out.

My mother, well versed in the art of careful housekeeping by my grandmother, was a dab hand at making little dresses for my sister and me from her own old frocks; curtains were restructured to fit different windows; and Christmas presents were often handmade. I know this sounds slightly like too much hard work by today's standards, but the 'carefulness' of the war years left a lasting impression on those who had lived through them, and the acquired skills of thrift and inventiveness enabled my mother to run a huge vicarage and growing family on the shortest of shoestrings.

I'm not suggesting that anyone should go back to living as we did in the postwar years of the 1950s and 1960s, and neither am I saying that these were particularly halcyon days, but the simplicity and carefulness of those years is perhaps something that we should aim for now in our complicated twenty-first-century lives.

Many of my clients who were children in the last war are now faced with the dilemma of 'to keep or not to keep'. They have the ingrained attitude that waste is bad, and so have lofts and garages full of defunct equipment and old furniture. They hang on to objects 'just in case'. They also have a lifetime of memories attached to their possessions. On the other hand, this generation has more disposable income than ever before, and so are enjoying buying new household items and upgrading their furniture and equipment. At a time when they should be downsizing with a vengeance, our older generations are experiencing a clutter crisis!

Don't be scared to let go

Many people find it hard to get rid of things because they are scared that they'll need an item as soon as it's gone. I understand this, but sometimes it's the *fear* of not having a thing that creates the sudden need for it. Subconsciously we want the very thing we no longer have, thus demonstrating to ourselves that we should have kept it after all. Louise Hay, author of many inspiring self-help books teaching you how to love *and* heal yourself, tells us not to be fearful of such things – 'the universe will provide'. Hay says that holding on to things shows that you have an inner fear that you won't be able to afford to provide for yourself in the future. However, there are very few things that you can't buy, beg or borrow again if you really need to. Don't be scared – just let your clutter go!

Filling a gap

Like compulsive over-eaters who are not really feeding their appetite, but the 'hole in their soul', so too there are compulsive spenders, trying to satisfy a gap in their lives through the temporary buzz that spending can bring. They quickly fill their homes with new purchases, but it's never enough to fill the gap.

I have worked with many people who have literally spent themselves into a corner. They are overwhelmed by stuff, but fearful of the pain of getting rid of anything. None of their purchases seems to bring them pleasure, and instead simply drives them still deeper into debt and clutter. Sometimes a person will know what his or her 'gap' is: maybe the desire for a special relationship, children, or a purpose in life, but for many this gap remains unidentified and their compulsive purchasing becomes a way of life.

Laura

When I first met Laura, she was 28 and worked in a shop, and had a seriously out-of-control spending and hoarding habit. Her whole house was filled with clutter; clothes and papers covered every inch of floorspace; countless carrier bags full of new purchases were piled in corners, as well as hundreds of unread magazines and unwatched videos, which formed part of an enormous and obsessive 'soap opera' collection.

When I visited her, Laura had reached an all-time low in her relationship with her parents, who were deeply upset at the way their daughter was living. She also felt unable to pursue a much-wanted relationship with a partner because she was ashamed of revealing to him how she lived. Added to this, she was struggling with a weight problem, an unfulfilled teaching career and depression.

All these created huge emotional gaps in her life that she was constantly trying to fill with her spending sprees. 'When I buy things, it cheers me up and promises me a fresh start,' she told me. 'I know I can't really afford it, but I think one more small thing won't make much difference.'

However, her obsessive spending *was* making a difference – she was deep in debt and didn't know by how much as she hadn't opened her bank statements for six months. Every new bag of shopping made her financial situation and her home mess worse, and pushed her relationships further and further away. Yet, even with her life in such a critical condition, Laura was unwilling to face up to her chronic overspending or get rid of her clutter. She became very withdrawn and angry during the de-cluttering session and said that she did not wish to continue.

Peeling off your layers of clutter and parting with possessions can often force you to face painful issues in your life. If you know that you are spending to fill a gap, veto all recreational shopping for a set period and aim to do some serious de-cluttering – both physical and mental. It might be time for you to seek counselling to sort out your emotional issues. Your doctor may be able to advise you of free counselling services, or if you wish to pay for private sessions, look in the Yellow Pages under 'Counselling and Advice'. (See the

British Association for Counselling in the Useful addresses section at the back of this book.)

Ask a friend to help you declutter, or seek help from a professional organizer. Check out the website for the Association of Professional Declutterers and Organisers (APDO) UK (<www.apdo-uk.co.uk>) or (in the USA) the Professional Organizers Web Ring (POWR) (<www.organizerswebring.com>).

Mental health and life issues behind the clutter

Depression

One of the most common effects of excessive clutter is depression. I often work with people who are depressed and sinking under what they have accumulated. Frequently they have cut themselves off from friends and family because they are ashamed of how they are living; they are only just hanging on to their job; and they are usually in a state of denial about how bad things have got. Their clutter surrounds them like a shell and their living space is usually reduced to one very small area of their house, like the sofa or the bed, from where they run their whole life.

Whenever I am called in to work with a client who has battened down the hatches against the outside world like this, I encourage him to take an active part in the de-cluttering programme, instead of just letting me do it for him. At first he may be reluctant, negative and sometimes even confrontational, but with lots of positive encouragement, he will get into the swing and may suddenly find he is quite enjoying it. Unlike counselling, when a client may have to focus on all that's wrong, this sort of therapy gives him the opportunity to make practical changes and focus on what he can do for himself and *get right* – that is, taking control of his space and enjoying restoring some order to his life.

Professor Kenneth I. Howard of Northwestern University in the USA is an expert on Cognitive Behaviour Therapy (CBT), which is often used in the treatment of depression and Obsessive Compulsive Disorder (OCD). He calls the first stage of CBT 'Remoralization' and says: 'Some patients are so beset by problems that they become demoralized and feel that they are at their "wits' end". This type of experience is pervasive and severely disrupts a person's ability to mobilize his or her coping resources. The person begins to feel frantic, hopeless and desperate.' This is a familiar feeling for many of my clients who have become overwhelmed by their own possessions.

Peter

Another of my clients was Peter. He was 50, divorced and very depressed. His life was not so much complicated as very stuck. He had been through two failed marriages, the most recent of which had resulted in an acrimonious divorce. He was very lonely and wanted a new partner in his life, but had not been successful in forming a new relationship. Although he had a good job, his real interest lay in the world of entertainment and much of his spare time was spent running events or appearing in shows. Although he had a lot of clutter, he had very few current personal possessions. What he did have dated back to his first marriage, had belonged to his children (now grown up) or had belonged to his recently deceased parents. There was no hint of his true personality in his home, only of his stage persona, which he put on when he went out.

Although Peter was being treated for severe depression, he was still unable to feel better or move on as he was quite literally stuck among other people's clutter from his past. He lacked the motivation to sort it out and found it painful to be reminded of people who he had loved and lost. This is often the case for people who are depressed. Inertia is part and parcel of depression, and knowing what you need to do is very different from being able to do it! Peter's house was in a terrible mess and was making him feel worse.

For our first session, Peter lay on his sofa all day, totally uninterested in taking part, and complaining bitterly about the whole process. At the end of the session, however, with my car full of stuff to take to charity shops, and the house more habitable, he told me that he felt a weight had been lifted from him and was keen to take part next time. During our second session he put up some shelves, took another car-load of stuff to charity and even made me a sandwich for lunch! The third time I visited him he had cut the lawn, planted up his window boxes, and had his conservatory cleaned inside and out. Proof that positive action can really help when you're feeling depressed, and that the more you do, the better you feel.

Seasonal Affective Disorder (SAD)

Seasonal Affective Disorder, sometimes called winter depression, affects an estimated half a million people and is caused by a biochemical imbalance in the hypothalamus due to lack of sunlight and short daylight hours. If you suffer from SAD, it can be really difficult to motivate yourself to get organized and stay on top of your clutter. You probably feel lethargic, anxious and miserable, and totally de-motivated.

Light therapy is known to be the best cure for SAD. (See Useful addresses at the back of this book.) Exposure to very bright light (ten times the intensity of ordinary domestic lighting) can improve the mood of the sufferer within a week. Some people buy or hire special light boxes, but just getting outside for a walk twice a day will give your eyes the chance to absorb as much natural light as possible and thus lift your mood. The exercise will be good for you too. Even if you don't feel like it – if you're down, just do it. It really will help.

Tiredness

Because being disorganized is so tiring, you may suffer from headaches or feel Tired All The Time (often referred to as TATT, or chronic fatigue syndrome). While symptoms are physical, the cause is usually non-organic and mostly results from circumstances that the person is living or working under.

Many adults suffer from chronic sleep deprivation without even realizing it. In the USA, sleep researcher Dr William Dement considers sleep deprivation to be 'a national emergency', affecting up to 95 per cent of adults at some time in their lives and resulting in stress, unhappiness and physical and mental exhaustion. The average night's sleep in the UK is now about 7.5 hours, while in 1920 it was 9.0 hours a night. The 2002 Sleep in America poll, conducted by the National Sleep Federation (NSF), shows that the average American adult now only sleeps 6.9 hours a night.

Some of the most organized people I know go to bed early, rise early and seem to achieve loads every day. Perhaps you wake up feeling exhausted and depressed, faced with a bedroom full of clutter and another day of chronic disorganization. My advice is to turn the television off early at night, get to bed at a sensible time, and aim to have the standard eight hours' sleep. Getting up early will be easier and you will give yourself a head start on the day. Making this one small adjustment to the amount of sleep you are getting could make a big difference to your feel-good factor *and* your self-organization. (See Useful addresses at the back of this book.)

Obsessive Compulsive Disorder (OCD)

Sally

Sally, 35, was moving house and wanted to get rid of her clutter before removal day. This is a normal request and I fully expected the usual moving mayhem, with boxes of stuff everywhere. Yet when I arrived I found that Sally actually had the smallest amount of stuff and wanted to reduce her possessions even more, so that everything she owned would fit into one large suitcase. Cupboards and drawers had been stripped bare, clothes were reduced to a minimal three outfits that hung on nails in the wall, and toiletries were pared down to a toothbrush, soap and flannel. In the kitchen she had three pieces of cutlery, a plate and a bowl, but when she said she wanted to reduce her mug collection to one, I suggested she keep both in case she ever had a visitor! Every surface was covered in sheets of kitchen towel to keep things clean, and she was very nervous in case I touched any of these areas and contaminated them.

Sally had Obsessive Compulsive Disorder (OCD), which affects 2–3 per cent of people in the UK today and is listed among the top ten most debilitating illnesses by the World Health Organization.

Her OCD had compelled her to get rid of nearly everything that she owned as she felt all her possessions were contaminated. She had reduced her living space to one room and had even taken her furniture apart so she was unable to use it. Even though she was totally free of physical clutter, she was unable to live a normal life. By making such drastic reductions to her possessions, Sally's life had become totally out of balance and she was living an impossibly Spartan existence. Finding the right balance in your life can be difficult and sometimes you may need outside help to do this. Visit <www.ocduk.org> or <www.phobics-society.org.uk>.

Other reasons why you might have too much stuff

Rewarding yourself

You've had a bad few weeks at work and wonder why you're working so hard for so little reward. You have a pile of bills, but there's a little voice in your head asking why you shouldn't reward yourself if you want to. It might be something as small as a new lipstick or as large as a holiday – but if you can't afford it, don't have it. Spending money you haven't got quickly leads to financial difficulties.

Boosting your self-esteem

You're feeling a bit down, everyone seems to be doing better than you, and you're generally dissatisfied with what you've got – these are all dangerous triggers for some serious retail therapy! By buying a recognizable status symbol, you are telling the world (and yourself) that you are doing well, even if you're not! Fast cars, big houses, designer clothes, expensive jewellery or the most up-to-date technology are all signals to say 'I'm OK'.

Sentimental attachments

Bereavement, the end of a relationship, or children leaving home – all of these can make us want to hold on to things to remind us of how life used to be. There's nothing wrong with looking back at happy times, and it's good to have special things to remind us of people whom we love. It's important to treasure the past, but just as important to live in the present and look forward to the future.

Saving things 'for best'

I helped an elderly couple to downsize their home, after 60 years of married life. The wife was going into a care home and the husband was to continue living independently, but in a small flat. As you can imagine, they had huge amounts of stuff to get rid of and it was a slow process. Emptying drawers and cupboards throughout the house I found endless items in brand-new condition, never used, having been saved 'for best'. Clothes, perfume, tableware, linen and more – all stashed away for special occasions and then forgotten about. It seemed very sad that these items, which could have given them pleasure, had never been touched. Don't save things for best – use and enjoy your possessions while you can. That's what they are for.

Too much choice

Do you ever feel overwhelmed by too much choice? Does it take you ages to choose something because you feel you have to look at everything before you make a decision? It's wonderful to have choices, but I am convinced that too much choice is a major contributor to a complicated life. For example, shopping in your corner shop is quicker and simpler than shopping in a huge supermarket because there is a limited amount of things to choose from. It might be a little more expensive, but you don't end up being seduced by goods and making unplanned purchases, so in fact you actually spend less money rather than more.

Don't compare yourself to others

Never compare yourself to others: they will always seem more perfect and successful than they actually are! Remember that everyone, no matter how successful and efficient they might appear to the outside world, is struggling in their own way and nobody is as they seem. Whatever you might see on the surface is not what is going on in private! This goes for me, you and everyone else. Think about the beautiful swans gliding effortlessly on the river. Not so – underneath they are paddling like mad just to stay afloat!

So don't set yourself impossible standards just because you think someone else is managing to do everything. They probably aren't! No one can do everything without missing out on something else. Trying to do *everything* means you will have to compromise certain areas in your life: either yourself, your family or your career. Decide on your own limits, know your personal threshold, and stick to it.

3

Assessing your situation

So you know that you want to make changes, but where on earth do you start? Well, you've already started, because you've made the mental shift. You know what direction you want to go in – now you just need to begin. Like any journey, the first few steps are the most daunting, but as you get into the swing of simplifying, it will become easier. So don't be hard on yourself and expect every area of your life to suddenly become more organized. Be patient and plan what you are going to do. Make the changes gradually, and over the space of a few months you will start to feel better – less stressed, lighter and more liberated.

You will need to deal with both your physical *and* your mental clutter. The two are inextricably linked, but you should deal with them separately. I would always advise dealing with the physical clutter first as this in itself results in more mental clarity. It's a bit like unblocking a sink and getting the water flowing again. Even if you don't manage to clear up the whole house at once (highly unlikely), one room alone is enough to (a) provide some energized space to live in, and (b) show how much better you will feel and encourage you to carry on and do more.

Planning

You may love or loathe the saying 'Failing to plan is planning to fail', but in this case it is entirely appropriate. Unless you live alone, have a planning meeting with the rest of the family before you start making changes. Your plans will affect everyone in your family, so it's only fair to let everyone know. You will also need to enlist their help if your change of lifestyle is to succeed. It's no good if you are the only one who thinks it's a good idea.

Find out what things you all enjoy and what drives everyone mad (and I don't mean Dad's personal habits!). Discuss if there are any things that could be done differently. Explain about having less stuff and how you think it will benefit all of you; find out if the rest of the family feel overwhelmed by possessions and mess, as well as you.

Talk about budgeting and discuss what each member of the family would be prepared to do to help cut back on spending.

Explain how and why you think it will help all of you. Make sure that they understand that you are trying to simplify your life to make it *better*, not to impose hardship on them. If you have children, don't forget to ask them if there is anything they would like to change, or do towards helping with the downshifting project. Never underestimate your children's input and capabilities – they might surprise you!

Start a 'snagging book'

'Snagging lists' are commonly used in the building industry. Towards the end of a construction project, the architect will go around the site, drawing up a list of all the small things that need finishing. The builders then work through the list, fixing all the outstanding items, and generally 'making good'. (In the USA, the term 'punch list' is used to mean the same thing.) I love the idea of snagging lists and use them a lot, both in my own home and when I work with clients. In a domestic situation they are a wonderful way of highlighting all those very small jobs that you mostly manage to ignore, but which, when added together, can really get you down. Dripping taps, doors that stick, wobbly tables, broken door handles, stained carpets – you know the sort of thing!

If you feel that your whole house is in turmoil, and everywhere you turn is in need of attention, don't panic! Control all those thoughts racing around in your head; get yourself a large A4 hardback notebook and make this your 'snagging book'. You are going to work through your home systematically, one room at a time, assessing exactly what needs to be done to make you feel better about your space and writing it all down in your book. Once you have committed your thoughts to paper you will have a plan to follow and therefore feel much more in control.

Sit quietly in the middle of each room in your home and view every inch of it with an objective and critical eye. Start in one corner and work clockwise around the room, writing down anything that you want to change, how it makes you feel, what bits you like, and which bits are truly awful. Is there furniture that is broken, can the clutter be reduced, are there any appliances that need fixing? Perhaps you hate the pictures, would like a new lampshade, or need to have the curtains cleaned. Maybe you could get rid of all the old videos, or your collection of ornaments that you no longer want. When did you last look at your room objectively?

Some things on your snagging list you will be able to fix immediately, others will take time. Don't jump up and start doing the easy things right away. Your task right now is simply to make a note of everything that you would like to tackle and not worry too much at this stage about how you're going to do things. Use your snagging list as a working guide for improving each room, and keep your main aim always in the forefront of your mind – that is, that you are aiming to *reduce and simplify.*

Remember that this is a *snagging* list and not an excuse for a *shopping* list! Of course, you may eventually want to buy new things as replacements, but even then I would encourage you to be strict with yourself and use only what you already have in the house. Need a new lampshade? Go and look in your loft – I bet you've got an extra one up there somewhere! Bored with the pictures? Swap them for the spare ones you've been keeping under your bed. Keep your eyes open for great household bargains at car boot or jumble sales, look in the small ads, ask friends and family, but whatever you do, just stay out of the shops!

Sample snagging list for your lounge

Immediate changes:
- Change 40 watt bulb for a 100 watt one for brighter light.
- Throw out dented lampshades and find replacements.
- Reduce books by 50 per cent – take to the charity shop.
- Aim for less surface clutter.
- Move all children's toys back to their rooms.
- Reduce ornaments – give to charity, sell or pack away.
- Chuck out all old magazines and newspapers.
- Get rid of the wobbly coffee table.
- Take down and rearrange pictures.
- Get rid of houseplants – too much maintenance.
- Change/wash cushion covers.
- Throw away net curtains and clean the windows.

Long-term changes:
- Dry-clean/wash curtains.
- Get the carpet cleaned.
- Wash the loose covers on the three-piece suite.
- Freshen walls with a quick coat of emulsion.

Examine your lifestyle

Each of us needs to live the very best life that we can, but we are often so caught up in the minutiae of existence that we don't listen to our inner selves. Look carefully at your life. Are you enslaved by your lifestyle? Are you working harder and longer just to keep your expensive car on the road? Do you belong to a gym, but never have time to go because you're always at work earning more money to pay your membership fee? Do your children really enjoy all the after-school activities, or are you just taking them because that's what the other mums do?

I am not preaching a Spartan existence or suggesting you give up everything you really enjoy, but start to be more aware of the areas of high spending and where you could simplify without too much effort. This will be discussed further in Chapter 6.

Know your own weaknesses

Being a fairly creative person I am a sucker for poor lonely old pieces of furniture that no one else wants, and can see the potential in just about anything. A lick of paint and a pretty seat cushion can give a new lease of life to a beaten-up old chair and many is the old picture frame I've rescued from a skip because I just couldn't bear to see it go to waste. People used to offer me things because they knew I'd take them, and it meant they didn't have to go through the real pain of getting rid of their own clutter – I took that responsibility on for them. What happened is that I ended up with a garage full of junk and became totally burdened with other people's clutter. Every time I went in my garage I was faced with DIY projects I knew I'd never get round to and it made me feel really bad!

I eventually got rid of all the never-to-be-finished furniture projects and became tough with myself. I learned to say 'no' when people offered me things, and even now I avoid the temptation of browsing junk shops and auction rooms in case my 'furniture-rescuing demons' rise up again! I'm telling you this because in assessing your situation, you must know your own weaknesses and defend yourself against them.

If you love shopping but can't really afford the time or money it takes up, and if your house and wardrobe are already full of stuff, then you need to start saying 'no' to yourself. Know your weakness – if it's shoes, stay out of the shoe shops, if it's CDs, don't browse the music shops, if it's books, use the library instead. If it's eBay, stay off the computer!

Having enough space

Any estate agent will tell you that you can never have too much space. Well, I think you can! We've all heard the saying 'Nature abhors a vacuum', and I'm afraid we humans do too! Give anyone a space and they will put their own things in it to make it their own. Even on the beach, we often stake our patch by placing a few belongings around ourselves.

Having more space means you can buy more stuff because you think you will always have somewhere to put it. But I have never come across anyone with enough wardrobe space, no matter how many wardrobes they have. They are always completely full. If you have space to keep things, then keep things is what you will do!

We will only get rid of things when we feel every inch of possible space is used up, so we have to be at 'full to bursting' point before our internal alarm bells go off. Everyone's threshold for fullness is different. Some people have a low tolerance to their own clutter, while others can let it pile up to shoulder height before they start to feel stressed by it. While you are assessing your home and lifestyle, take a look in all those dark storage spaces where things go to be forgotten. Pull stuff out that you haven't seen or missed for years and get rid of it. Decide to use the space properly, instead of just a place to bung things when you can't be bothered to think about them.

Renting storage space

One of my clients was so addicted to acquiring stuff, and felt so compelled to keep it, that when she had filled her tiny one-bedroom flat to capacity, she rented storage space elsewhere and filled that too! I worked with this client intermittently over several years and knew that she was spending a lot of money maintaining a large stash of clutter that she had no real use for. Eventually I persuaded her to deal with it and we spent a day sifting through her hidden hoard. Most of it was paper and went into the recycling lorry; the rest was rubbish. So after two years of prevarication, and several hundred pounds of money wasted, my client got rid of her extra storage.

Renting storage space is a very useful short-term solution, but should not be regarded as a permanent answer for keeping clutter. If you don't have space to use something in your home, what is the point of paying to keep it elsewhere? Work out the total cost of storage and compare it to the total value of the items you plan to store. If the storage is more expensive than the items, then think seriously about getting rid of them.

Me

As I mentioned earlier in the book, I am a professional organizer. I am married, with two children.

Several years ago, at about the time that I started my organizing business, I made a conscious effort to simplify our family life. I'd spent nine years at home as a full-time mum, bringing up the children and doing small jobs during school hours to bring in extra money. I had friends who had maintained their well-paid careers, but who envied me my stay-at-home life. In turn, I was envious of their status and salary and felt diminished by my lack of professional standing. But I realized that 'having it all' is almost impossible, and that trying to do everything almost inevitably means compromises.

I loved the challenge of starting a new venture from scratch and found it personally rewarding. However, it took up far more time than I had anticipated, and what had started as a part-time project seemed to require full-time effort. I was constantly tired and stressed, always late, always rushing the children around to various activities, and never doing anything properly. This wasn't how it was supposed to be!

I also owned a lot of clutter myself, having been an avid collector of items from junk shops since I was a teenager. Although it had been fun building up my collections over the years, I didn't really need them any longer and felt I had outgrown all my stuff. So I made some new rules for myself. I assessed every area of our home and family life and decided what had to go in order for the new business to run comfortably alongside the rest of the family. This is what I did:

1 I did a major de-clutter so there was less stuff to look after.
2 I stopped all after-school activities for the children – they were delighted!
3 I said 'no' more often when people asked me to do things.
4 I stepped down from the committees I had been serving on.
5 I gave up charity work and instead gave a cheque equal to my fundraising efforts.
6 I stopped ironing anything but the absolute essentials – we all still looked OK!
7 I only did chores one day a week, usually on Sunday.
8 I stopped high-maintenance gardening.
9 I stopped doing anything I didn't really want to do.
10 I stopped feeling guilty about all of the above!

These changes weren't drastic and didn't have a negative impact on anyone. However, they were enough to provide me with the time and space to attend to my business without compromising my family. Once I had made these decisions and decided not to feel guilty about them, I found life was much less complicated and consequently less stressful for all of us.

Identify your space stealers

Every cluttered home that I visit is different, but most present the same types of clutter, in varying amounts.

My Top Ten space stealers are:

1 Paper.
2 Books.
3 Ornaments.
4 Unused electrical appliances.
5 Too many clothes.
6 Crockery.
7 Household linen.
8 Toys.

9 Unloved furniture.
10 Gadgets.

Identify your saved 'junk' items

These are the items that I most often see saved by people. They are not intrinsically useless, as I know many are re-usable, but some people save stuff obsessively, without considering a sensible limit. If you collect used postage stamps for charity, send them off every six months. If you collect mini shampoos from hotels, for heaven's sake use them – otherwise what's the point in having them? If you've amassed hundreds of old greetings cards, cut them up for gift tags or use the fronts to send as postcards. Don't just save them for the sake of it.

The Top Ten most commonly saved 'junk' items that I see are:

1 Microwave-meal containers.
2 Yoghurt pots.
3 Bits of wood.
4 Used postage stamps.
5 Carrier bags.
6 Hotel/airline freebie shampoos, etc.
7 Bits of cardboard.
8 Pieces of material.
9 Used envelopes.
10 Old greetings cards.

Hoarding

Whenever I give a public lecture there are always people who come up to me afterwards with their own hoarding stories. One lady told me about her husband's giant ball of string which stood 70 centimetres high and had reached antique status! It had been passed down from generation to generation for at least a century and consisted of hundreds of pieces of string knotted together into one continuous piece. Of course, he would never use it, said his wife, but he had kept it because he didn't know what else to do with it.

In my work I often come across secret hoards of strange things. Again, the older generation is ever thrifty and saves string, brown paper, butter wrappers, buttons, elastic bands, plastic bags, etc. There's nothing wrong with this and I wish more people would recycle and re-use in this way. It's just that sometimes the hoarding instinct goes a bit out of control and we end up hoarding things for no particular reason, other than that we can't bear to throw something away. If you know you are a bit of a hoarder of 'useful stuff', set limits for yourself and have an annual sort-out to keep it under control.

So, to recap. In assessing your situation, you need to:

1 Examine your lifestyle, spending and possessions.
2 Plan which areas you would like to simplify.
3 Start a 'snagging book'.
4 Know your weaknesses.
5 Stop making excuses.

As one of the easiest ways to simplify and revitalize your life is to have less stuff in it, in the next chapter I am going to talk in detail about de-cluttering.

4
Getting started

I always make a preliminary visit to a new client before I start working with him, so I can see his home, understand the nature and severity of his clutter, and try to get to know him a little. I tend to work intuitively with a person and the time spent getting to know him at the beginning is invaluable to me in really being able to help him deal with his clutter successfully. Something I nearly always find is that the client is totally paralysed by the enormity of the simplifying task.

'There's so much mess everywhere I just don't know where to start,' one person said to me. 'As soon as I start one area I get distracted by something else that needs to be done and I just end up moving things from one place to another without really dealing with them. Although I start off with good intentions, I just don't seem to make any progress and then I get despondent and give up. In fact, I usually make my clutter worse by moving things around so then I decide not to bother even trying.'

This is all too familiar and I am certain many of you reading this will relate to it. I agree, when there are numerous things clamouring for your attention, it's extremely hard to remain completely focused on clearing one small area, but not impossible.

Like many people, I too find it very difficult to think clearly, work effectively or make any major decisions when my physical space is in turmoil. (Yes, even professional organizers can get in a mess sometimes!) Although I always try to practise what I preach, sometimes family life, and the details of running a small business from home, get the better of me and stuff builds up.

Feeling stuck

A few years ago I reached just such a hiatus, in particular with my business, and I felt very stuck. Although things were ticking over in an average kind of way, I knew that I was simply treading water and not making any progress in certain areas of my life. Working from the corner of my dining room was not good for me. I seemed to be surrounded by half-finished projects, each with its own pile of related paperwork; I was sitting next to the hamster cage, squeezed in between two packing cases (still untouched since our recent house move), and trying not to look at the ironing basket or mending pile on the floor at my feet.

I knew which direction I wanted to go in with my business, but was having great difficulty getting there! I found I couldn't concentrate and was spending a great deal of time achieving very little. I had no clarity of thought and just felt confused and ineffective. I knew that the problem was my cluttered working space, but just didn't know where to begin. I was completely bogged down by inertia and got into 'can't be bothered' mode.

One morning I woke up and decided that I couldn't stand being like this any more. I looked around for the thing that made me feel my worst when I looked at it, and knew that was where I would start. It didn't take me long to find it. In a corner of my dining room was a box containing 1,000 leaflets that I'd had printed, at great expense, when I started my organizing business. Two years and one house move later, my leaflets had the wrong telephone number, no web address, and didn't really reflect what I now wanted to say. As a marketing tool they were useless, but I had spent a lot of money having them printed and I felt bad about getting rid of them. I realized that I felt worse keeping them than I would throwing them away – so out they went, and finally I stopped feeling so stuck.

Once I had made the decision on the leaflets, I was on a roll! The matching business cards also went and the paper with the old letterhead was given to the children to draw on. I then went through all my files and chucked out any papers I didn't need any more; I aimed to get rid of about a third, but managed almost half. Patting myself on the back, I then felt brave enough to look inside the two packing cases and decided that all of what was in them could go to charity without being missed. I found a new home for the ironing basket, spent half an hour catching up with the mending, and poor old Digger the hamster got sent back to my daughter's bedroom, whence he had come.

The whole process took me about half a day and resulted in a much clearer work area for me, both physically and mentally. Suddenly I found it easier to focus my thoughts and was able to see the way forward with my business. By clearing the physical clutter I had also given myself some mental space. My advice to clients who are similarly stuck is always 'just start'.

TOP TIP: If you are overwhelmed by too many tasks, or paralysed by indecision, focus on one small thing to begin with and the rest will follow. My difficulty had been finding the small thing to get me started, but as soon as I did, the rest was easy.

Procrastination

A common trait of 'clutterbugs' is that they are great procrastinators and will take all sorts of evasive action to put off the scary moment when they eventually have to decide what to do with their stuff. You will often find clutterbugs browsing the storage aisles in stationery stores or DIY centres, looking for magic purchases that they hope will rescue them from their clutter. But guess what? Only they can do that for themselves. No amount of ready-made solutions will work if you still can't bring yourself to get rid of anything. You will continue to have the same amount of stuff.

Finding the right storage

Every overloaded person I meet seems to have a penchant for purchasing useful storage and organizing items. Their homes are bursting with plastic boxes, filing trays, stationery drawers, and desk tidies – many still in the original wrappings, usually empty and just adding to the general mess. Some people misguidedly think that the more storage stuff they buy, the more organized they will become. Not so. The more storage stuff they buy, the more cluttered they get. Buying new storage and organizing items simply puts off the evil moment when you have to deal with your clutter.

In my experience, most people already have plenty of adequate storage solutions in their home. Reduce and simplify your possessions, cull your clutter, and you will find that you suddenly have space for things, using the storage that you already own.

Finding the time

Many people don't get round to sorting out their stuff because they say they don't have the time. They don't consider it's important enough and they have a hundred and one other things to do first. Believe me, getting the other hundred and one things done will be a lot easier once your space is sorted, so I strongly recommend that you move de-cluttering and organizing straight to the top of your 'To Do' list.

If you are really struggling to find time, then have a designated 'De-cluttering Day'. Do it at the weekend and, if you live with family, enlist their help, or take a day's leave from work during the week and go it alone when the house is quiet.

On the designated day, don't be tempted to go shopping, invite anyone round (unless they're going to help), do the ironing, watch daytime television, or get lured by any other diversionary activities. Turn the answering machine on, roll up your sleeves and get stuck in!

Your essential de-cluttering and organizing kit

One of the best things about de-cluttering and organizing is that you don't need any fancy equipment to do it. It's one of the most inexpensive forms of therapy I know and you might even end up making a bit of money from it if you have items that you can sell. (See Chapter 10.) When I work on a major de-cluttering session with a client, I always find the following items useful:

- *Plastic crates with lids.* These are an exception to my 'no shopping' rule and are top of my organizing list. Clear plastic crates are the best as you can see what's in them and lids are imperative as they keep the contents clean and dust free. Boxes with lids are also stackable and easier to move about. This is one of the few occasions when I would advise you to buy in bulk; get a range of small, medium and large. They are readily available in most large DIY and stationery stores, as well as homeware departments of large supermarkets.
- *Sturdy cardboard boxes and duct tape.* Useful for when you take all that stuff to the charity shop or box it up for a car boot sale. Make sure your boxes aren't too large or you won't be able to lift them when they're full. Put several strips of tape in both directions across the bottom of the box before filling it, especially if you are putting heavy items in it.
- *Shoeboxes.* These are optional extras, but can be very handy. They are free (ask any shoe shop), stack easily on shelves, and can be covered with gift wrap if you want a co-ordinated look.
- *Black plastic sacks.* Use heavy-duty ones – the cheap thin ones rip too easily. If you have more than one sack on the go when you're

de-cluttering, don't forget to label them clearly so you know which ones contain rubbish and which ones contain items for charity.

- *Self-adhesive labels.* Plain white labels are essential for your organizing kit, preferably peel-off ones. Buy a range of sizes and a black marker pen for writing on them. Label all storage boxes, rows of files and crates so you can see at a glance what's where. If you are setting up a new storage system for the rest of the family to use, labelling is a must.
- *Jam jars with lids.* Have a matching set for paperclips, rubber bands, drawing pins, string, etc. They can look quite chic standing in a row on a shelf.
- *Stapler and hole punch.* A heavy-duty hole punch can go through about 12 sheets at once and save you loads of time when filing large amounts of paper. If you need to attach a few pieces of paper together, use a stapler, not a paperclip. Paperclips can easily attach themselves to something else, or fall off. A staple is more permanent.
- *Cardboard folders.* These are useful to sort different projects into as a first approach to getting your papers sorted.
- *Ring binders.* If you really want to get your papers under control there is nothing more satisfying than a shelf full of labelled ring binders. They are inexpensive to buy and, in my view, the best way to organize your papers.
- *Bulldog clips and plastic sleeves.* Simple solutions are often the most effective ones. My organizing kit would not be complete without a big handful of bulldog and fold-back clips in various sizes. They are brilliant for holding together things like receipts, or a large stack of paper prior to filing.
- *Plastic file inserts.* I like the transparent plastic sleeves that you buy to put in folders. They are really useful for sorting many things, and provide a quick solution if you need to organize photos, cuttings, recipes or receipts, but you don't have much time. You can seal the tops with a bit of tape if there are small, loose items such as photos that may fall out. I use these plastic sleeves a lot for big paper-organizing projects, but in some cases they are only a temporary solution until the ideal permanent one is found. However, they are a great starting point for the divide-and-conquer approach to paper-taming!
- *Shredder* (see Chapter 5).

A word of caution

Never, ever use a paper spike for holding papers. They are highly dangerous. A few years ago a friend of mine was standing on a chair to reach a high shelf in her office. She slipped and fell on a paper spike which went straight through her wrist. Very fortunately, and amazingly, there was no lasting damage to her arm, but a sharp spike sticking upwards is a very dangerous way to organize your paper.

The power of one

Always concentrate on one thing at a time. Pick a room and select an area in it that you are going to work on. It could be one drawer, one cupboard, even one file. Don't allow yourself to become diverted into other areas – keep focused on this one task, however tempted you might be to start something else.

Even doing one small area every day will result in steady progress, as long as you continue to concentrate all your efforts on the same room. Don't flit to other rooms or start other projects. Keep looking back at the progress you have made and don't allow panic to creep in when you look at how much there is still to do. Slowly but surely is the order of the day!

Trying to sort out too many areas at once is precisely the reason that so many people are unsuccessful at de-cluttering and simplifying their homes. One client e-mailed me to say she had been working on her bedroom, her kitchen and her garden shed, but didn't really seem to be getting anywhere. My advice was to stop flitting from space to space and concentrate all her efforts on one room only. A week later she told me that after concentrating her efforts successfully on her bedroom for a day, she had done the same in the kitchen, and was now finally working on the shed.

TOP TIP: Stay focused on one area at a time.

Where to start

Refer back to your snagging lists. You have critically assessed your situation and by now will know exactly what room in your home makes you feel the worst, although I'm sure you already knew!

There may be some rooms that don't need too much attention – perhaps only a minor clear-up. When I start work with a new client we will always de-clutter and organize the easiest room first, as a kind of warm-up and to encourage them. This may only take an hour or two, after which you can stand back, admire your work, and congratulate yourself. Hooray! You can cross out one whole page in your snagging book. You have passed the first milestone to a simpler life. Close the door and move on.

Reward yourself with a cup of tea and a sticky bun – yes, seriously! Tea breaks are very important when you are de-cluttering. You are expending a lot of energy, both physical and emotional, and you should take plenty of ten-minute breathers throughout the day.

If you are working in a confined space and not moving around very much, which is often the case, then remember to go outside in the fresh air every hour or so to stretch, breathe deeply and walk around a bit, just to get your circulation moving. If you are working in a particularly dusty area, such as a loft or garage, it's a good idea to wear a paper mask over your nose and mouth, to protect yourself from breathing in too much dust and dirt. You can buy these inexpensively from most good DIY stores.

Ready, steady, go!

Before you start, make sure you have boxes and bin-bags ready labelled so that you can sort stuff as you come across it. I have known some people go to the extreme of hiring a huge skip and chucking absolutely everything out, but this is a terrible waste and we should never add unnecessarily to landfill. I know that most people would prefer their stuff not to go to waste and, with a little planning, you *can* dispose of things conscientiously.

Label your boxes as rubbish, recycle, charity, keep, shred

1 *Rubbish*. This is all stuff that is unloved, unusable, broken, has bits missing, and has only narrowly escaped being thrown away many times before. Now is the time to finally get rid of it.
2 *Recycle*. Most local authorities operate comprehensive recycling facilities, much of it in kerbside collections. Although it varies from area to area, we can now recycle paper, cardboard, glass, certain

plastics, and even green waste. So before you chuck things in your rubbish sack, ask yourself if it can go in your recycling box. Check your local council's website to find out what goes where. (See Useful addresses for unusual items to recycle, e.g. batteries, paint, furniture, tools, computers.)

3 *Keep*. You will undoubtedly come across items you wish to keep which belong elsewhere in the house. They need putting back in their rightful place, or you need to find a new place for them. Don't do it now, there is a real danger that you will get diverted. Put items in a box labelled 'Keep' and deal with them later in the day. Don't be like one of my clients who went to put a CD back in her son's room and was gone for half an hour. When I went to find her she had started reorganizing his CD collection!

4 *Returns*. You may find things you have borrowed that need returning to their rightful owners. Keep a box or basket near your front door and put all outgoing items in it as soon as you come across them. You may also find things that you wish to pass on to others. Although it's good to do this, don't make it an excuse for not getting rid of things. Many clients that I work with spend ages trying to think of someone who 'might like it' when really it's just another way of putting off the moment of parting with their beloved clutter. It's also making someone else take responsibility for your stuff, which isn't fair.

5 *Charity*. I'm often surprised when people ask me what items they can donate to charity shops. The answer is almost anything as long as it's in good, saleable condition. Most charity shops take clothes, jewellery, books, toys, unwanted gifts, and household goods, although they are unable to sell electrical items due to health and safety legislation. Many charities also collect and recycle old mobile phones and printer cartridges (see Useful addresses).

6 *Shred*. Don't waste time shredding personal papers now. Just throw them all in a box marked 'Shredding' and have a major shredding session later. (There is more on shredding in Chapter 5.)

Work from one side of the room to the other and handle each item only once. Pick it up and ask yourself the following:

- Do I use it?
- Do I love it?
- Do I have a logical place for it?

- Could I manage without it?
- Could it be replaced easily?

If you don't love it and you rarely use it, then you can definitely manage without it. If you want to keep something, you need to find a logical place for it so you can find it when you need it. Unless an item is unique or of great sentimental value, most things can be replaced.

De-cluttering can be quite slow to start with and you will probably spend ages deliberating over even the smallest things when you begin. This is often the case when I work with clients, but I know they will speed up as the day wears on. The continual decision-making process – 'keep or throw', 'yes or no' – gets quicker and the importance of items diminishes when you are faced with volume. By the end of the day you will be chucking out like a champion, your boxes will be full, and space will have started to emerge.

TOP TIP: Take 'before' and 'after' pictures of your space to remind yourself how bad it was before and how fantastic it looks afterwards.

Things can only get better

One of my grandmother's favourite sayings was 'It's always darkest before the dawn', and I think of this every time I am helping a chronically cluttered client do a major sort out.

When everything has been pulled out of cupboards and drawers and spread out to sort, the room can look worse than ever. The more we get out, the worse it looks, and after a few hours I sense my client's spirits taking a steep nose-dive. He gets agitated and short-tempered and I know he is bitterly regretting having started. This is the point of no return. I happen to know that it's also the 'tipping point' – that crucial, pivotal point where everything is about to change. I am aware that my client is shortly going to feel excited and relieved when he sees order and space emerging, and it's really important to keep going through this feeling of despondency. I give him lots of encouragement and tell him it's all going brilliantly, which of course it is!

If you are de-cluttering on your own, be aware that you may feel like this. Remove rubbish from the house as soon as bin-bags are full and put your charity shop boxes straight into the car. Bag up your recycling, label it, and put this outside too. Keep clearing up as you go along so you're not falling over rubbish all the time and you don't get confused and overwhelmed by bin-bags and boxes everywhere.

As soon as you have cleared some space, clean it! Get a damp cloth and wipe away all the dust. Vacuum any carpet that hasn't seen daylight for months. Clean skirting boards and banish cobwebs with a feather duster. Only then should you start to put stuff back in place. Sense your house heaving a sigh of relief and breathing again after being so full of stuff for so long. Feel your energy levels rise and your optimism return.

Finding it tough to let go of stuff?

If you're finding it hard to let go of stuff, ask yourself these questions:

- If the house burned down, would I rather lose my stuff or my loved ones?
- Do people like me because of who I am or what I own?
- Will owning fewer things make me feel any less of a person or will it make me feel less burdened and more whole?
- Does all this stuff really make me happy?
- Why am I frightened to let stuff go?

TOP TIP: The more you de-clutter, the less important your possessions will seem to you. Just keep telling yourself 'It's only stuff'! The most important thing is to start.

5

Home admin – day to day

It's often a build-up of the smallest things that can make us feel the least in control of our lives. Boring as it is, the minutiae of existence cannot be avoided. Most people need to work, cook, shop, wash, look after their home, maybe look after others, deal with finances and paperwork. If you stop doing any of these things, a backlog will build up and this can quickly impact on all other areas of your home admin.

Sometimes you may have a big project that takes priority, such as decorating, or a work deadline to meet. At such times, normality seems a long way off and you think you will never get straight again, but you will. However, I believe it's most important to reduce your home admin to its simplest form so you don't add unnecessarily to your stress levels by always looking for papers, losing your diary, missing appointments, forgetting to pick up the children and other such errors that occur when your mind and your admin are in two separate places!

Your household HQ

Running a home is no mean feat and, as such, it deserves its own designated operations centre. If your household and family admin is normally done from the corner of the kitchen table, make it a priority to get your own desk, bureau or workstation. Having your own workspace is a major step towards being more organized and in control when you are running a home and family.

Keep your in-tray here, all papers relating to the children and school, important documents such as passports and birth certificates, and any other household paperwork. In every home the division of paperwork is different. In our house I handle everything to do with children, school, social life and all things domestic, while my husband deals with everything financial. Neither one of us would interfere with the other's area – the odd time this has happened, things haven't run smoothly! Old-fashioned as it may seem, it works for us, although I admit it may not work for everyone. However you

42

divide up the responsibilities in your home, make sure both you and your partner understand what each of you is expected to do.

If all the household admin falls to you, then it's even more important that you have a clearly defined paperwork area. You don't need to spend a lot of money on a flashy desk, just as long as you have a small space to call your own and a place to keep your paperwork and files. One of my clients converted a wardrobe cupboard into a very efficient little operations centre, complete with shelves for files and room for a simple work-surface where she could put her laptop. She did need to have a major purge of her wardrobe in order to make room for this, but, in doing so, killed two birds with one stone; she ended up with a de-cluttered wardrobe and her own small office space.

Home admin tasks

Finding time to keep up with paperwork and admin is a big challenge for many people. Let's face it, shuffling papers around is not the most exciting task, and if you don't have much spare time, it's tempting to keep moving it to the bottom of your 'To Do' list. However, staying on top of things is the key here, and 'little and often' is far better than 'huge amounts, infrequently'.

TOP TIP: Make a will – a surprising two-thirds of us haven't, but to die without one causes so much heartache and hassle for our loved ones. (For information about making a will, look under the excellent website <www.ifishoulddie.co.uk>.)

Use an in-tray

This should *not* be used as a receptacle for unopened post, magazines, keys, bits of shopping or broken toys. It is purely for pieces of paper that need dealing with. So *after* you have opened your post, put into your in-tray bills to pay, bank statements to reconcile, forms to fill in, letters to answer and the like. Nobody is able to deal with everything immediately, but even if you only get round to dealing with your in-tray once every two to three weeks, you will still be on top of things. My husband and I have regular admin days when we both catch up with our outstanding paperwork.

It's a bore, but once it's done, we always feel brilliant, and really in control.

Opening post

Strange as it may seem, I often need to show clients how to open their post! Any mail that comes through the door is potentially going to add to your paper mountain. Most of it is uninvited and should end up in your recycling box. Cull incoming papers daily and aim to reduce your mail to its bare minimum. Keep your recycling box near where you open your mail. When you open your bank statement, throw away the envelope and the three advertising leaflets that come with it. All you need to keep is the statement. Don't put everything back in the envelope and just leave it on the hall table as so many people seem to do.

Open everything, even the stuff that doesn't interest you, and make immediate decisions on whether to keep it or throw it away. Don't open junk mail. You didn't ask for it, you don't want to buy anything from the company, so just bin it!

Opening and reducing your mail in this way shouldn't take more than three or four minutes. If stuff needs dealing with, it can go in your in-tray for you to deal with at a later date. Don't be like one of my clients, who receives up to twenty items of post every day but only ever opens the ones that look of immediate interest. Therefore every six months he accumulates several crates of unopened mail that then take a whole day to deal with.

Diaries

Make it a rule to put dates in your diary *immediately* you know about them. Never rely on your memory. If you have a busy family life it's important to have one master diary for the whole house in order to avoid double bookings. Have regular 'diary sessions' to make everyone in the family aware of what everyone else is doing.

If you and your partner both work and don't have time to sit down and do this, simply e-mail each other or write notes with any new dates – the important thing is to keep each other informed. Leaving notes for each other might seem a little formal, but this system works well for my friend Petra whose husband travels extensively and whose presence at home is, to say the least, unpredictable.

Confirm dates immediately

If someone asks you if you're free on a certain date and you don't have your diary with you, don't agree to the date before checking. Say you'll ring them to confirm as soon as you've checked your diary, then do it *immediately you get home* before other things overtake you and you forget.

Accepting invites

If you are able to attend an event, reply to the invitation as soon as possible. Should your attendance depend on having a babysitter, book the babysitter first and then reply to the invite.

'House meetings'

Hold regular 'house meetings' for everyone in your family, when you can sit down together and discuss what's going on. Cover anything you like – work commitments, menus for the week ahead, holidays, homework, etc. Allow everyone to have their say and use this as a forum for resolving any family squabbles. You can also discuss fun things you'd like to do: films you want to see or places you'd like to visit. Keep your house meetings short or your children will hate them, and make sure that everyone follows up any actions that have been agreed.

Keep it simple

Don't set up over-complicated systems for yourself. Like strict diets, complicated systems are hard to stick to and easy to give up.

Some people have invented systems that are impossible to use. One of my clients had arranged such a complicated cross-referenced filing system for herself that even *she* wasn't sure where to file things, and certainly wasn't able to retrieve anything once it had been put away. Eventually, confused and fed up that her system wasn't working, she stopped filing anything at all and simply piled all her papers up in a corner of her office. It took several days to sift through the paper mountain, sort papers into obvious groups, and then set up some simple alphabetical files for her.

TOP TIP: Always keep systems simple; complexity rarely results in efficiency.

'To Do' lists

If you feel like you're running around all day and not achieving much, focus yourself with a 'To Do' list. I'm sure you know what a 'To Do' list is, but I'm often surprised at how many people don't use one. Each day make a list of all the things you need to get done, no matter how small. Add to it as things pop into your head – you may remember something while you're brushing your teeth, sitting in traffic or cooking the tea – *just write it down*! Don't rely on your memory. If you are feeling tired and stressed, your memory is one of the first things to let you down.

Cross things off your list as you do them. This might sound obvious, but don't forget to do it because it's a great visual reminder of how much you've achieved in a day and will make you feel really good. If you haven't managed to do all you'd hoped by the end of the day, it doesn't matter. Get into bed and write out a new list for tomorrow, carrying forward any outstanding items that didn't get done today. You'll sleep better if you've emptied your mind before putting the light out.

TOP TIP: Stick to one list at a time. I know some people who are great list-makers, but who confuse themselves by having too many lists. For simplicity, work from one list only and carry it with you at all times.

Use a 'daybook'

Have a 'daybook' for all your ideas, notes, lists, jottings or interesting information. This is much better than lots of bits of paper floating about, which are easy to lose. If you do scribble on a scrap of paper, stick or staple it into your book. Put a sticker on the front of your daybook with dates 'from and to' and also number old daybooks chronologically to make them easier to keep in order on the shelf. Your daybooks can be a great source of reference when you are trying to remember things from months ago or if you need to look up a name, date or telephone number. I always carry an A5

46

spiral-bound notebook for lists and notes; it's small enough to fit in a handbag, but big enough not to lose, and I never leave home without it.

Notice board

Have an events notice board in a central place in your home, ideally above or near your household HQ desk. Use this for all paperwork associated with upcoming events or appointments, such as appointment cards for the doctor or dentist, party invitations, travel itineraries, theatre tickets, flyers for events. Throw away paperwork once an event has passed. Regard this notice board as one of your organizing tools and don't let it become cluttered with unnecessary paper such as postcards, recipes, photos or newspaper cuttings.

Weekly planner

Buy a wipe-clean weekly planner, and fill it in every Sunday evening with everyone's activities for the week ahead. If you have children, it's especially useful for keeping track of childcare arrangements, lift-sharing and after-school activities. Schedules can get complicated, particularly if you are a working parent, so writing things down helps to clarify arrangements for everyone.

Shredding

Many of the people that I visit are worried about getting rid of personal papers because they are fearful of identity theft. This is one of the UK's newest crimes and, disconcertingly, 'bin raiding' is on the increase. In a survey commissioned by Experian (2005), a provider of fraud prevention solutions, it was revealed that 75 per cent of local authorities in the UK admitted that bin raiding takes place in their area, and that the problem is getting worse.

Experian found that many consumers discard significant quantities of financial information such as credit or debit card numbers or bank account details that, in the wrong hands, can be used for transaction fraud and identity theft. Only 14 per cent of household bins contain no information of interest to fraudsters.

I agree that we should take these findings seriously and exercise caution when throwing personal papers away. However, many people are so fearful of identity theft that they are almost drowning in paper.

If you've been meaning to buy a shredder but not got round to it yet, put it at the top of your 'To Do' list. I recommend buying a good-quality home shredder for around £80, sturdy enough to take about 12 sheets at a time. Don't bother with the little plastic desktop shredders – they are wholly inadequate for the job. Keep your shredder accessible, near your desk or where you open your post. Do it there and then, or set up a 'shredding box' and then have a big shredding session at the end of the week. Generally, shred anything with your name and address on it: envelopes, postcards, receipts that may carry financial information, old utility bills, letters and, most important of all, old bank, building society and credit card statements.

Magazine boxes

I use these with many of my clients who want easily accessible storage systems for papers that they use on a daily basis. The boxes sit easily on a shelf, look good in a row, and are great for storing magazines, catalogues, school papers, exercise books and many other floppy paper items that fall off shelves too easily. If I had to choose my top three organizing tools, the catalogue box would be one of them. Cardboard ones are inexpensive and effective, but you can spend more money and get sturdier plastic or even leather ones if you like. However, to get organized on a budget, I would always advise going for the cheaper ones first and then buying better ones later, once you know the arrangement that works best for you.

Recycling boxes

No matter how tight on space you are, recycling boxes should have a place in your home. Try to find a location for at least one box and throw in cardboard packaging, paper, tins and plastic bottles. Wash tins and food containers to avoid unpleasant smells – most of this will be hand-sorted at the recycling depot, so spare a thought for the sorters!

Although more people than ever are now recycling, there are still those who think their own small efforts won't make any difference to the grand scheme of things. Wrong! Here in the UK, we currently need to be recycling or composting 25 per cent of all our household waste, in line with EU targets, with this figure rising to 30 per cent by 2010 and 33 per cent in 2015. Check your local council's website for details of what the kerbside recycling collections will take and then *do it*!

Get the rest of your family involved – I've always found that children are brilliant at rising to a challenge and taking responsibility. In our house, my ten-year-old son is our chief recycling officer and is responsible for washing and squashing all cans and plastic bottles, and taking organic kitchen waste out to the composting bin in the garden. It's a great idea to set a family goal for reducing the amount that goes in your bin – you'll be amazed at how much less you can put out for the rubbish men when you really try.

Gardens

- If you can afford it, pay someone else to do garden chores.
- Go for low-maintenance plants.
- Don't allow yourself to be seduced at the garden centre by gorgeous plants that aren't going to survive neglectful treatment. Beware 'child in the sweet shop' syndrome! Don't make impulse purchases!
- Give old garden furniture a new lease of life with a good wash-down, a lick of pretty outdoor paint, and some inexpensive new cushions. Don't feel you have to buy new furniture.
- Up to a third of all household waste is biodegradable and suitable for composting, and many local councils now sell composting bins at a discounted rate. Even if you only have a small garden, there should be enough space for a simple composter.

Have a permanent charity bag

Keep a large carrier bag in the bottom of your wardrobe or in a cupboard. Whenever you come across something you no longer wear, read, love or use, throw it into the bag. As soon as the bag is full, put it in the car and drop it off at the next charity shop that you pass.

Cleaning, laundry and other household chores

It's much easier to keep your home clean when you have less stuff in it. Surfaces are easier to wipe when they are empty and floors are easier to sweep and vacuum when not cluttered up with things. If you feel you spend too much time on cleaning and other chores, you may need to drop your standards a little. I'm not suggesting that you suddenly give up all cleaning and laundry, but just ask yourself if it really matters that the house is less than perfect, or that the family have to wait a bit longer for clean clothes. Allow the children to help you, even if what they do is less than perfect. Give them jobs that they can manage such as pairing up the socks, putting clean laundry back in drawers, sorting the whites from coloureds, etc.

Will you ever regret not doing enough cleaning or laundry? Probably not. You may, though, regret not spending time doing the things you really wanted to do.

Laundry

Put a dirty washing basket in every bedroom and bathroom so nobody has an excuse for leaving dirty clothes lying on the floor. Let it be known that if things aren't in the basket, they don't get washed. Tell everyone in your family that if they want something washing urgently, they should put it on the floor near the washing machine and *tell you*! You do not read minds, although you can do almost everything else!

Peg out more

Can't be bothered to peg out the washing? Take a look at your electricity meter while your tumble dryer is on! It will be whizzing round! Save yourself money by pegging out your washing whenever you can. Bring shirts in when they are slightly damp and they are easier to iron. Take the trouble to peg out – enjoy the simple pleasure of a line full of washing blowing in the breeze and thinking how lovely it smells when you bring it in.

Reduce your ironing

Don't make work for yourself! If you're using your tumble dryer, then smooth and fold items such as children's T-shirts, school sweatshirts, nightwear and sportswear as soon as they come out of the machine. Don't leave them to cool with all the creases in. Try and peg out items so that they dry in shape and therefore need less ironing. Shirts can be hung on plastic hangers and then dried on the line.

Fold duvet covers, pillow cases and flat sheets smoothly as soon as they come out of the washing machine and dry them folded on the radiators (in winter) or on the line in fine weather, not in the tumble dryer. Iron them while still folded so you don't need to iron every side.

Never, ever iron socks, underwear or towels!

Mending clothes

Be old-fashioned – have a mending basket. Loose buttons, fallen hems, ripped seams – pile them up and do them all in one go. If you're hopeless at sewing and you know you'll never get round to it, find a friend who *can* sew and offer to do a free babysit, or some other favour, in return for an hour or two of sewing time.

TOP TIP: Home administration is not a finite task, but an ongoing process. Reduce it to its simplest form by being as organized as possible and dealing with things immediately that they arise. My advice on home admin is simply 'Stay on top of it, so it doesn't get on top of you'!

6

Finance and 'things'

Working closely with people who are in clutter crisis I get to see a lot of very personal things. Paperwork in particular quickly reveals what is going on in a client's life. When I am sorting papers at speed I tend to just scan the contents to decide where they should be filed, but red bills and 'overdue' letters always jump out at me. The more credit card statements I open for a client, the more I know they are spending large amounts on unnecessary stuff. The more unopened post there is, the more likely it is that my client is in a financial mess and has gone into 'ostrich mode', sticking his or her head deep in the sand and hoping the money problems will go away.

I do not write as an accountant or financial expert – there are plenty of publications devoted to managing your money effectively (see Further reading at the back of this book) – but there are two simple rules re money:

1 If you haven't got it, don't spend it.
2 Know your limits and stick to them.

I don't want to be a killjoy, but I believe shopping really is the 'root of all evil' as far as clutter is concerned. *Stop shopping*! If you are trying to simplify your life, I recommend that you stop *all* shopping for a period of, say, three months, apart from the absolute essentials, of course, such as food, loo rolls, etc. Your bank balance *will* increase and your clutter *won't*!

It's really very comforting to give yourself permission *not* to spend money for a while and to make do with what you already have. It also saves you loads of time that you would otherwise have spent trudging around shops looking for things to buy.

Some common money traps

1 The lure of mail order
The majority of my most cluttered clients are avid catalogue shoppers and spend a fortune on stuff that they don't really need, although they truly believe that they do. When I try to persuade them

to get rid of their catalogues in order to help them cut down on their spending, they become very anxious in case they don't have the opportunity to purchase these particular items again.

Everyone enjoys a wander through 'catalogue-land', but it's a dangerous place to go! I would advise that you flick through your catalogues as soon as you get them, but then bin them. The whole point of a catalogue is that it seduces you into wanting things you never knew you needed! Ask yourself if you can live without these items and don't be conned into placing large orders just to save on postage. Why spend £40 just to save £3.50 in postage, when you could actually save yourself £43.50 by throwing out the catalogue?

2 Supermarket seduction

There is a whole industry built upon how you, the shopper, behaves in a supermarket. Although you may not know it, you often buy exactly what the marketing experts intend you to buy! They plan which way you are going to walk around the store and set up tempting displays on the ends of aisles to ambush you and your wallet when you're least expecting it. One minute you're doing the grocery shopping, the next you find yourself with lacy lingerie and a couple of CDs in your trolley! *Caveat Emptor*! (Buyer Beware!)

If you're doing the food shopping at a supermarket, be strict with yourself. Don't be diverted into the clothes section or browse through the CDs and homewares, no matter where your wayward trolley might lead you! Unplanned browsing will not only eat into your time, but will also increase your expenditure, as you will almost certainly end up making impulse purchases! If possible, shop without the children so you're not inveigled into buying all sorts of rubbish, food or otherwise. Stick to your list, and if you can't find something, survive without it! Buy what you need, not what you think you'll need. Does it fit into a meal or school lunch? If not (i.e. if it's just snacks), leave it.

3 Gym/health club membership

Do you make a charitable donation to your local health club every month? That's what you're doing if you have a gym membership but never go. Work out how often you *really* go to the gym each month and then divide that number into the cost of your monthly membership. If you're looking at a cost of something like £10–£15 per visit, then you are wasting your money. You are probably a reluctant gym user and you would be better off simply walking, swimming or going to a keep-fit class once or twice a week at your local leisure centre.

4 Incidental eating out

Resist the urge for a quick cappuccino when you're out shopping, or taking the children for a burger and chips because they missed lunch. Casual snacking like this quickly erodes your cash and you've nothing to show for your spending apart from an empty wallet! Mealtimes at home are much cheaper, and better for your children too. If you can't avoid being out around mealtimes, then take things with you for the children to eat. Fill old lemonade bottles with water or squash so you don't have to buy drinks, and take snacks.

5 Buying in bulk

Bulk buying only works if you have somewhere to store all your purchases. If you have to live surrounded by loo rolls, giant boxes of washing powder and crates of dog food, then shopping in this way doesn't necessarily make your life simpler, it just makes it more cluttered. One of my clients buys all her household products in bulk from a cash & carry warehouse. She says it saves her money, but she has nowhere to put anything and so stores her bulk buys in the loft – not the most convenient place to find your next loo roll! Because her house is so full, this lady needs to rent storage space elsewhere and so the money saved on bulk buying is gone. Unless you have a utility room or dry garage with plenty of storage space, let the shop store bulk items for you.

Buying in bulk can also make you less frugal in your usage. For example, if I buy a giant 24-pack of crisps, my children will pig out, but if I only buy a 6-pack, they will be far more careful in their consumption.

6 Cash & carry warehouses

Don't be fooled into thinking that these vast warehouses are cheap. Many places display their shelf prices without VAT. Take your calculator with you and add on the VAT to discover the total amount you will be paying. You may find that the special offers at your local supermarket are actually better value.

7 Cheap stuff

There is a place in my very organized heart for bargain basement-type stores! They always sell a fantastic range of storage and organizing solutions at rock-bottom prices and are like Aladdin's Cave, full of interesting bits and pieces that you never knew you needed! The danger of these stores is that they pile stuff high and sell it cheap and we buy far more than we need, just because we can't resist a bargain. I have a friend who spends a fortune in these shops and her house is full of tacky rubbish. She thinks she's saving money by buying this stuff, whereas in fact she is spending more than normal.

8 Charity shop bargains

Gone are the days when you could pick up things cheaply in a charity shop. I applaud the rise of charity shops as seriously well-run boutiques, but am disappointed that in many areas they have out-priced themselves. If you love browsing round charity shops, beware how much you can spend – three items of clothing can easily set you back £15 or more. One of my clients was so addicted to buying charity-shop bargains that she had bags full of purchases that she had never worn or used. When I helped her de-clutter her bedroom, most of these items went straight back to the shop she had bought them from, ready priced! If you can't resist making purchases in charity shops, avert your gaze when passing the window and move swiftly on.

9 Magazine subscriptions

Review your magazine subscriptions. Do you just let the standing order continue from year to year without even thinking about it? Do you sometimes never even remove the mags from their plastic wrappers? Do you really read them or just flick through? Save yourself money by cancelling all your subscriptions and only buying magazines as an occasional treat.

One of my clients was a keen motorcyclist. He subscribed to several specialist bike magazines and had huge stacks of old copies going back about five years. He also ran several businesses and simply didn't have time to read the magazines. Most of them remained in their plastic wrappings and joined the ever-increasing pile at the bottom of a cupboard. I suggested that he cancel all his subscriptions and just buy his magazines individually from the newsagents as and when he wanted them.

10 Entertainment and socializing

Being sociable can be expensive – eating out, babysitters, takeaways, drinks with friends, cinema trips, they all add up. Keeping a written record of all such spending for two to three months will show you exactly how much money trickles away unseen on these things. Of course, it would be a very dull life if you suddenly cut out all entertaining and socializing, but I believe this is one area you can cut back on without too much hardship. Limit takeaways to one a month, wait until films come out on DVD instead of going to the cinema, don't call in for 'a quick drink' on the way home from work, forgo the theatre visit. Invite friends round instead of going out, and ask everyone to bring food to share.

Children and money

1 Pocket money

Once children get to a certain age, they inevitably want pocket money. It's hard deciding on the correct amount for the right age, but whatever weekly amount you decide to give, it's a good idea to keep a note of it. Buy a little cashbook for each child and write down the amount given to him/her each week, and the date. A parent must initial the book to show they have paid the money. Pocket money may be accrued and paid in arrears, so the cashbook acts as a kind of savings scheme.

This might sound a bit over-the-top for 50p or £1 a week, but it is early money management and is a good way of teaching your children to look after their money and also to save up for something if they want it.

2 Saving for children

Teach your children the rudiments of saving. Explain to them in the simplest terms about banks, building societies and interest rates – we need to make sure our next generation is more money-wise and less hand-to-mouth. One weekend when my children were quite young, my husband Gareth, who has always been brilliant at explaining difficult things simply, decided to teach the children how money works, and set up a little 'bank' in the dining room, with himself as cashier. They learned about writing cheques, paying in money, earning interest, and having an overdraft – and thought it was the best fun ever!

If your children don't already have savings accounts, take them along to a building society to open one. They will enjoy having their own names on their passbooks and will be able to pay in birthday and Christmas cheques for themselves. Watching the amount go up every year is very satisfying, especially when the interest is added.

3 Teenage bank accounts

When my friend Nick's daughter turned 13, he opened a bank account for her. Then, instead of giving her pocket money in cash every week, he paid an allowance into her account. He taught her how to use the cashpoint machine, how to write a cheque, and how to pay money in. She had no overdraft facility and quickly learned not to overspend. When the money was gone, it was gone – there was no more until the next month. She really enjoyed the responsibility of handling her own money and making it last from month to month. This may not be the right thing for all children, but it can provide a bit of controlled financial independence for growing teenagers.

4 Peer pressure

As a parent of teenage children, I often feel torn between my desire to please my kids and my wish not to be part of the consumer trap. When they were small I used to shop at car boot sales and charity shops if I needed something for them. Not exclusively of course – I like buying new things as much as anyone – but if I could avoid buying new I would. It was cheaper, didn't support the consumer/ manufacturing loop, and was better for the planet. My children were none the wiser and never lacked for anything.

Now, however, my children are older and wiser about what's 'hip' and what's not. They know exactly what you should or shouldn't be seen wearing or carrying. Mobile phones, trainers, clothes, console games and more – all are important status symbols for today's young people.

Like many parents, my limited income has to stretch ever further, to buy yet more for my children, in order to keep them afloat in a competitive consumer peer group. Even so, whatever I buy is never enough and they are always looking for the 'next big thing'. There always seems to be a residual dissatisfaction with today's children. When they get what they wanted, they look over the fence to the next field, see the grass is even greener there, and then want that instead. I don't think this means that children are particularly selfish or greedy; they are just growing up in a 'have-it-all' society.

As a parent trying to live a simpler, less expensive life it can be difficult trying to rein in the spending all the time when your children want you to spend ever more. Resist, resist! You will be doing them an enormous favour by *not* giving in to their every whim, and their short-term resentment will, hopefully, eventually be replaced by a healthy understanding of the value of money.

Tips to stay in control of expenditure

1 Budgeting

If you lack organization in other areas of your life, it's likely that your money and spending isn't very organized either, so as part of your overall reorganizing project I would advise that you start some simple budgeting.

Get a small notebook and write down *everything* that you buy so you can work out *exactly* where your money is going. If you seem to make a lot of cash withdrawals, this is the best way of finding out where your cash is going. Track your spending meticulously for a week and you will see how a magazine here and there, bits of dry cleaning, the odd bunch of flowers, and miscellaneous purchases from the local shop can quickly erode your cash. Make a conscious effort to cut down on the casual daily spending and you will notice a difference in your wallet and ultimately your bank balance.

Allow yourself only a certain amount of cash every week and see if you can make it last. Whatever amount you withdraw from the bank you are likely to spend it, so limiting the amount is a good idea. If you are used to drawing out £50 a week, get £30 instead and make it last.

If you know that your spending is high in certain areas, such as clothing or entertainment, set yourself a monthly budget and stick to it. Sometimes *not* buying stuff can give you as much of a buzz as buying it, especially when you realize how much you *haven't* spent in a month.

TOP TIP: If money burns a hole in your pocket, then only ever leave home with the smallest amount. You will indulge in fewer impulse purchases and won't be able to fritter it away on snacks, newspapers and other sundries.

2 Track your spending

When I work with clients who feel their finances are out of control, one of the first things I suggest is that they keep track of their daily spending by saving all receipts. The best way to do this is to set up a series of large A4 envelopes, labelled chronologically with the month and year. Keep receipts for everything you buy and put them into the envelope when you get home. At the end of the month add up how much you have spent in various areas such as food, clothes, entertainment, petrol, etc. Paperclip receipts together in each category and write the totals on the front of the envelope so you know how much you are spending each month. This is an excellent way of tracing where your money is going and can help you to identify areas of high spending. It's also handy to be able to lay hands on receipts if you need to return faulty goods to shops.

You might think all this sounds a bit labour-intensive! I agree, compared with the fun of shopping, it's rather tedious, but it forces you to get your head out of the sand and look at what you're spending your salary on. You should have a good idea of where your money is going and this might be the wake-up call you need. Most people are shocked by their own spending when they do this exercise.

3 Saving receipts

One word of warning about receipt saving. One of my clients had kept receipts obsessively for the last 25 years and had boxes full of them. For her, these bits of paper had become sentimental items in themselves, reminding her of things she had bought when she was first married, clothes she had worn, etc. Don't go down this route; a receipt is a receipt – it's just a bit of paper. If you are self-employed and the receipts show business expenses, then you should keep these for seven years, but otherwise don't keep receipts for day-to-day spending for more than a few months.

Another of my clients had got into the habit of keeping all her receipts because she wanted to check off her spending against her bank statements. With a backlog of several years of unchecked receipts and two young children taking up all her time, I knew that she would never get round to this mammoth task, but she insisted she would. When we costed in her time for doing all this checking, it worked out at hundreds of pounds, probably far more than she would have saved by discovering even one bank error!

This is meticulousness gone wrong. When you get so far behind with an obsessive task like this, there comes a point where you simply have to draw a line and start again. So what if you've lost a bit of money? Is it worth all the hassle to sort it out? I used to fight such things to the bitter end, but now I always put a price on my time, effort and angst and find it's often simply not worth it. I don't want to waste my time fighting and feeling bad and therefore much prefer to shut up and move on. (See Further reading for full details regarding the book *S.U.M.O. (Shut Up, Move On)* by Paul McGee.)

4 *Be a meanie*

There's one very easy way to save money – stay away from the shops! See if you can last a whole week without visiting the supermarket *or the bank*! Live frugally for a while. Make yourself survive on what you have in the fridge, freezer and store cupboard. Most people have more food than they think.

Go through your bathroom cupboard and dressing table drawers and get out all toiletries that you've been given. Make it a rule to use all these up before you go out and buy anything else. And if you're running low on toothpaste or shampoo, make them last a bit longer by storing them upside down!

There are many other areas of your home where you will have resources that you can use up before buying more. If you have a drawer full of birthday cards or gifts, use them. Consolidate all the pencils, pens and paper lying around the house, and again you will find there is more than enough to keep you going for quite a few months. Being frugal doesn't mean you have to go without, it just means you have to be more economical – and organized. Just make a point of using up things that you already have before you buy more.

5 *Keeping financial papers*

You should keep bank statements, payslips, P60s, receipts, tax documentation and other financial papers for seven years, particularly if you are self-employed. Archive these papers in clearly labelled and dated boxes. Separate them into tax years, or chronological years if you prefer. Keep papers from the last two years in an accessible place and store the rest.

6 Pay-back time

If you borrow cash, pay it back quickly. You might forget, but the person you borrowed it from won't. If it's a small amount, they might be too embarrassed to ask, but it will niggle at them and make you look bad in their eyes. If you have difficulty remembering this sort of thing, then write it down. Don't say 'you must remind me' to the other person – it's *your* responsibility to remember, not theirs.

7 Find the best deal

There are always better deals to be had – you just need to take the time to find them. Mortgages, loans, utilities, mobile phones, insurance; look carefully at how much you pay for each of these. Take time to shop around and you may save yourself several hundred pounds over the course of a year. Read *The Money Diet* by Martin Lewis.

7

Protecting your time

Time is your most precious commodity and needs protecting as much as your space. When you're young you treat time casually, wishing the days away, feeling bored, wanting to be older, wanting a more high-profile job so you can buy more things. Once you're older, with the high-profile job and all the trappings, all you want is more time and you start to understand phrases like 'Cash rich, time poor'.

Owning too much stuff has a direct link to not having enough time. The more things you own, the more things you have to look after, move around, and tidy up. The less you own, the more free you are. If you are someone who never has enough time, perhaps you should look at exactly how you are spending it, to highlight where your time is going and help you be more aware of wasting it.

How do you spend your time and energy?

Everyone has the same amount of time per day, but we all choose to spend it differently. If you are working a 40-hour week, it's because you choose to do so. If you have to work long hours to pay a huge mortgage, it's because you chose to have one. If you have young children to care for, it's because you chose to have them. Life is about choice. Even if you think you don't have any choice, you do. Everybody has choice.

Do you spend a lot of time commuting? Do you waste time and money on recreational shopping when you could save both by not going into town? Do you work long hours to support a lifestyle that you don't particularly enjoy? Would you be happier with less money if it meant that you had more time?

Michael
Michael lived with his wife in a huge and very beautiful Victorian country house. They had no children, and although the house would have made a wonderful family home, it lacked ambience and had an uncomfortable stillness about it. Both Michael and his

62

wife were keen collectors of antiques and had worked hard to fund their valuable collection of paintings and porcelain. Beautiful as it was, I found their home to have a very draining atmosphere, and after working there for a whole day I felt totally exhausted. The energy in their home was completely stagnant and, almost in support of this, even my watch stopped working while I was there, starting again as soon as I got home.

I knew that if I felt like this after only a day in the house, Michael and his wife probably felt the same, only worse. I discovered that Michael's wife was in fact very depressed, but felt trapped and powerless to make changes. She and her husband had to continue working to pay the mortgage, insurance and huge household bills, which included staff wages, as the house was too big for them to look after on their own. They had chosen to spend their time at work in order to fund their home, which, although fabulous, was far too big for the two of them and was not a source of happiness.

Stop trying to do everything!

Don't feel that you have to do *everything*, no matter how much pressure you feel you are under. Simplify your life by saying 'no' when people ask you to do things, instead of agreeing to something now and then regretting it later. Ignore the old adage 'if you want something doing, ask a busy person'. (This must surely have been invented by some work-shy person who wanted an easy life and no responsibilities!) If you are that busy person, say 'no'! You are probably already fully loaded with commitments, so why make it worse by taking on even more tasks? Allow yourself some slack and don't fill every minute of every day. Put some 'white space' in your diary so you have extra time to catch up if you need it.

Top Ten 'time-thieves'

1 Watching television

In a recent study, Dr Aric Sigman, of the British Psychological Society, said that by the age of 75, the average person in the UK will have spent more than 12 years of full 24-hour days watching television. 'There's nothing to be lost by watching less TV, but a great deal to be lost by continuing to watch as much as we do,' he said. Adverse health affects linked with television viewing range from obesity to Alzheimer's disease.

Buy a television viewing guide every week (or save money and print off daily viewing schedules from the internet), and mark the programmes you *really* want to see. Give yourself a viewing allowance of one or two hours a night, and aim to keep one evening television-free. Stop aimless viewing and channel hopping. Don't turn the television on unless it's to watch one of your chosen programmes, and make a point of turning it off after your programme has finished so you don't get drawn into the next one. As an experiment, make a note of how many hours you spend watching television in a week and try to reduce this by at least one-third.

Enjoy doing something else instead of watching television and see how much more productive your evenings can be when you get up from the sofa and press the 'off' button. One of my clients decided that she would unplug her television for a week and use the time she normally spent on viewing to go through her backlog of photographs, sort them out, and get them all into albums. Most people tend to put off a large task like this because they say they don't have time. In fact, we *do* have time but we need to be more selective about how we spend it.

2 Surfing the internet

Apart from watching television, one of the biggest technological timewasters is 'surfing the net'. Limit yourself to 30 minutes a session – use a timer if necessary. If sites are taking ages to load, come back to it later when there is less internet traffic, don't just sit there waiting.

3 The phone

The phone (landline and mobile) can be an intrusion and an interruption and interfere seriously with your time management. You may be running late, in the middle of a meal, washing your hair or putting the children to bed. If it's simply not convenient to answer the phone, then don't! Let your answering machine take your calls for you – that's what it's for – and return calls when it's convenient for you.

Use a cordless phone so you can do something else at the same time as talking, such as ironing, washing up, or cooking. Or use e-mail where possible – it saves time by avoiding 'telephone tag' or getting involved in time-consuming conversations.

Make notes of phone calls when speaking to shops, businesses, suppliers or tradespeople – jot down who you spoke to, the date, what was agreed and any action that needs to be taken. Don't rely on your memory. Attach your telephone notes to any relevant paperwork, and file at once.

Don't allow nuisance sales calls to waste your time, either. Have you ever dropped what you're doing and rushed to pick up the phone, only to find it's someone wanting to sell you something or asking you to take part in telephone 'surveys'? Just politely say 'no thanks' and hang up.

4 Chatty friends

Do you have chatty friends who take up too much of your time when they ring? Do you pick up the phone and your heart sinks? Ask them to hold on a minute – go into the kitchen and set the oven timer for 10 or 15 minutes (however long you are prepared to listen to them). Stand near the oven so that they will hear when it goes off. Tell them you have to go because the meal is ready. If you don't have an oven timer, just open the front door and ring the doorbell – 'Really sorry, but I've got to go, there's someone at the front door.' It works every time!

5 'Flaky friends'

Do you have a particular friend who only ever wants to see you when things are going wrong in her life? Do you spend hours hearing the same old problems and giving advice that you know will never be taken? Does your friend only ever talk about herself and never want to know about you? This is a 'flaky' friend, and one who will waste as much of your time as you are prepared to give. Get rid of any one-way friendships that sap your time and energy, especially those where you have nothing in common any more. Spend your time with people who you want to be with, and don't let others use you as a free counselling service.

TOP TIP: Spend more time with the ones you love by spending less time with the ones you don't!

6 Saying 'yes' when you mean 'no'!

Often in the past I have volunteered to do something and then later wished I'd said 'no' when I find it eats into our family time, or into something else I need to do. I have been out for evenings when I would have preferred to stay at home, simply because I didn't like to say 'no'. I have spent whole weekends with old school friends because I thought it would be rude not to. I am sure these examples are not unique to me and you can probably think of many occasions when you too have said 'yes' and regretted it!

If you often find yourself saying 'yes' to things that you'd rather not do, but you're worried about what people will think if you say 'no', it's time to toughen up. Your time is as precious as the next person's so you shouldn't have to spend it doing things you don't want to. Learn to say 'no'. If you really don't want to do something – don't!

Don't let other people erode your time. Get rid of some of your mental clutter and commitments. Step down off the committee, say 'no' more often, and examine how important a friendship really is to you.

> TOP TIP: Don't be afraid to say 'no'. By saying 'no' to others you say 'yes' to yourself.

7 Lie-ins

What a wonderful feeling to allow yourself to wake up naturally, without the alarm clock, and then to lie in bed knowing that this time is yours. How lovely to get a morning cuppa and the newspaper and snuggle back down for a lazy lie-in. I think lie-ins are a necessary part of resting our bodies and recharging our batteries, but if you spend all weekend lying in bed, it's a huge waste of time. Let a lie-in be a special treat and not the norm.

8 Recreational shopping

This is a favourite pastime and a favourite time (and money) waster too! Many people love a bit of 'retail therapy', and I agree that it can be fun. However, you can waste hours doing recreational shopping – which is entirely different from the more mundane grocery shopping – and still come home with nothing or with unplanned purchases that you don't really need. Limit yourself to one browsing session a month.

9 Washing and ironing

Of all the regular household chores, washing and ironing probably take up the most time. A UK National Government Statistics Time Use Survey (2000) showed that in the average UK household, of the total time spent in laundry/clothing-related activities, women did 85 per cent of this, while men contributed only 15 per cent. The survey also reported: 'Females spent more than twice as much time on ironing than males spent in total on clothing related activities'! (No surprise there then!)

Have you ever picked up an item of clothing off the floor and thrown it in the laundry basket even though it might not be dirty? Are you simply creating extra washing for yourself? Not everything needs to be washed after only being worn once. Try to wear things for longer and ask the rest of your family to do the same.

A small mark on the front of something might easily be removed with a damp cloth instead of going through the whole wash cycle. Your clothes will survive longer with less washing and you will use less water, washing powder, energy and time. If each person in an average family of four were to reduce their items of washing by one a day, that would be one load less to do each week and 52 loads less a year. Think how much time that would save you!

10 Worrying

I once read that worry is like a rocking chair: it keeps you going, but gets you nowhere. Worrying is the least productive and most time-wasting activity on Earth. Did you know that 95 per cent of the things that we worry about never happen, so what's the point in wasting time worrying?

There are some people, however, who are consumed with anxiety about everything, to the point where their extreme worrying can result in an illness known as Generalized Anxiety Disorder (GAD). People with GAD will even worry about worrying – they can't stop irrational negative thoughts going around in their heads and, in the most severe cases, they may be unable to lead a normal life because of their fears. (For more information on GAD and useful websites, see the Useful addresses and Further reading sections at the back of this book.)

Ten ideas for protecting your time

1 Know where to find things

Make sure that all important things in your home have a designated place so that you don't waste time looking for them, especially just as you are about to leave the house. For example, your car keys, handbag, mobile phone, cheque book, passport, driving licence, diary, etc. all need to be kept where you can find them immediately.

2 Buy in some help

I am always surprised by the number of people (especially women) who struggle along trying to do everything on their own, because they think buying in help is extravagant. If you are working hard to earn more money to have a better life, spend some of that money on making your life simpler and getting rid of some of your mundane household tasks. Buy yourself some leisure time. Don't view hired help as an extravagance – it's a necessity!

3 Don't be late

Those who are habitually late are usually those who try to cram too much into their schedule. Don't allow occasional accidental lateness to become your normal *modus operandi.* While friends are usually forgiving of occasional lateness, business colleagues may not be. It shows a disregard for others and implies that your time is more valuable than theirs.

If you're someone who is well known for lateness, then redeem your notoriety by using an alarm to keep you on time. Your mobile phone probably has one, your oven too. Or buy a small travel alarm clock or kitchen timer – very handy if you are shopping and don't want to run over on the parking meter. Need to collect the children from school? You have a business appointment or meeting with a friend that you're worried you'll overrun? Set your alarm.

4 Don't overload your time

Never underestimate how long anything takes. When arranging appointments, domestic or business, give yourself plenty of time between each one, and however long you think anything is going to take, add on an extra 30 minutes. This allows for slippage, and if you finish on time you will have an extra half an hour to sit and read, catch up on phone calls, do a quick bit of (essential!) shopping or fill the car up with petrol.

5 Completions

Don't hop from one thing to the next – always try to complete things before moving on to another project. Keep focused and stay with a task even if it gets boring, otherwise you will end up with lots of half-finished jobs and no satisfaction.

One of the most common shared traits of all my cluttered clients is that they are serial project-starters, but terrible completer/finishers. Their houses are full of half-finished projects. They won't put things away because they say they'll come back to them later, but then something else seizes their interest and they abandon the first task in favour of the new one. Little piles of unfinished things build up all over their house. Stuff acts as a magnet for more stuff, and soon it's out of control. If you're not a 'completer/finisher' by nature, you'll probably have all sorts of excuses for not doing things.

If you have half-read books or partly completed craft projects you've got bored with, just move them out of your life – donate them to charity or give them to someone else who will enjoy them. Hanging on to them will remind you what you didn't manage to get done and make you feel bad.

TOP TIP: Make a list of all outstanding tasks that need dealing with (no matter how small) and work through them before you allow yourself to start anything new. Finishing one task at a time is much more time efficient than trying to do several things at once.

6 Working from home

This means you have to be very disciplined with your time. It's easy to be diverted with domestic tasks when you have a less than interesting piece of work, and you are easy prey for friends who drop round for a coffee or ring for a chat.

Decide on your core work hours and stick to them. If you find this hard, then make appointments with yourself in your diary so the time is blocked out for work.

7 Long-term commitments

If you want to stop a long-term commitment but don't want to let others down, just tell them. They may be feeling the same! Dropping one or two of your regular commitments can free up significant amounts of time and you will immediately feel the pressure ease in other areas of your life.

One of my friends continued to meet with her antenatal group every month for years, until her children were teenagers. She didn't enjoy it, and when I asked her why she just didn't stop doing it, she said she felt bad about breaking up the group. Although this commitment had been right for her when her children were small, it had become an unwelcome obligation over the years. Never feel obliged to continue a commitment that you really don't enjoy, simply because you think you should.

TOP TIP: Recognize when you have grown out of a commitment. Change is good. Move on and reclaim some of your time.

8 Waiting time

Waiting is one of those irritating things that we all have to do sometimes. There is nothing more annoying than sitting in a traffic jam or a doctor's waiting room watching the minutes tick away and thinking of all the things you could be doing instead. Unfortunately, you have no control over such situations, which is stressful in itself, but try to view waiting time as a bonus instead of a nuisance. Use it profitably by catching up on stuff you wouldn't normally have time for.

Perhaps you are the family 'taxi driver' and regularly spend time sitting in the car waiting for your children. Maybe you have to accompany elderly relatives to hospital appointments. If I expect to be waiting somewhere, I take the pile of newspaper articles with me that I have set aside 'to read later'. I also carry a notebook with me at all times to jot down thoughts and ideas when I have an unexpected spare moment. A teacher friend uses her waiting time for marking exercise books, another takes her laptop and prepares lessons. You could read a book without feeling guilty, write your next 'To Do' list, sew on name labels, listen to books on cassettes, catch up with correspondence or make phone calls. You could even (and here's an idea) just sit quietly and do some thinking!

TOP TIP: Have small portable tasks ready to take with you when you know there are going to be spare minutes to fill.

9 Procrastination

Many people have a tendency to procrastinate over unpleasant or boring tasks. Things that you repeatedly put off can quickly become mental clutter and hang around in your head. The longer you leave them, the worse they get.

Most mental clutter consists of niggling worries related to outstanding tasks and actions. Mental clutter fogs your thinking and prevents you from moving forwards. The unresolved items just sit there at the back of your mind, bothering you, but once they're dealt with, the relief is so great you wonder why you didn't do them before!

If you have decisions and appointments that you need to make, people to see, payments to send or letters to write, *do them now*! Make a list and work through it. Many items can be dealt with in a phone call or e-mail and then they have been cleared from your head.

TOP TIP: Empty your mental in-tray and stop wasting precious time procrastinating.

10 Accepting help

Reduce your standards to increase the level of help you can receive.

If you have children, allow them and your partner to help around the house; don't keep all the tasks for yourself because you think no one else can do them as well as you. Nearly everyone I know who has a 'cleaning lady' says they could do it better themselves, but just ask yourself, 'Is it good *enough*?' Waiting until you are on the verge of a nervous breakdown before asking your family for help will only result in them telling you 'you only had to ask' and wondering what you're making such a fuss about! If you're a perfectionist you will destroy yourself, as you think no one else will ever do anything as well as you can, and you will probably drop dead with exhaustion after multi-tasking yourself into a corner. Allow yourself some slack. Nobody ever died of a slightly less than perfect house!

Children's tasks might be:

- Vacuuming.
- Tidying.
- Dusting.
- Car washing.
- Ironing.
- Sweeping up outside.
- Wiping down paintwork.

There is no reason why your children shouldn't help with household chores but, if they are reluctant, a little bribery works wonders! Keep a small pot of loose change so you can pay them immediately for tasks completed. If you have a large family and really want to make a thing of this, keep a tally of who has done what and have a 'Helper of the Week' bonus prize. Line up some really easy tasks so that even very young children have the opportunity to do their bit. Kids love the task/reward system and it's a great motivator for them. I would not advocate payment for *everything* – setting and clearing the table, keeping a tidy bedroom, unpacking school bags and putting dirty clothes in the laundry basket are all tasks that your child should do as a matter of course. And remember, quell the critical perfectionist in you and resist snatching the vacuum cleaner from your child's hand, even if he's missed a bit! The best way for children to learn is by letting them do things. They will only get better with practice.

Ten-minute tidy

Have you ever noticed how much you can get done in the shortest space of time if you really have to? Like those mad moments when a friend rings to say she's in the area and can she drop round in ten minutes for a cuppa; you might be frantic for ten minutes, but the result is surprisingly good! Work on the 'ten-minute tidy' principle and give yourself this much time every morning for a quick tidy and wipe-down in key areas such as the kitchen and bathroom. Before you leave the bathroom after your morning ablutions, give the sink a quick clean, put a squirt of bleach down the loo, and wipe round the loo seat with a disposable disinfectant wipe. Clear the kitchen surfaces, put the breakfast dishes in the dishwasher if you have one, and yesterday's papers in the recycling box. It might not be a deep cleaning process, but it'll keep you on top of things and save you from getting behind as the week goes on. Set yourself small challenges like emptying the dishwasher before the kettle boils, peeling the potatoes before the next two songs have played on the radio, or finishing the ironing before your favourite television programme starts.

> TOP TIP: Ten-minute tidy sessions are a great way of getting the children to tidy their rooms. Tell them they have to get as much as possible done in ten minutes, set the timer, and see who has the tidiest room at the end of it.

'Bubble bursters'!

I use the phrase 'bubble bursters' to refer to those people and activities from whom you need to protect your time, your ideas and yourself.

There are times in life when you review what you're doing and realize that time is ticking away and you haven't achieved as much as you'd like. You may decide that you need to make some changes, do something different or embrace new challenges – in short, make the most of your time. Sometimes we are ready to take the plunge and step outside of our normal comfort zone to try something new. It might be an adventure holiday, a career move, starting a business, or simply realizing a long-held ambition.

Catherine

One of my clients, Catherine, had spent 18 years as a dutiful wife, mother, church member and voluntary worker, and decided that her fiftieth birthday would mark a turning point in her life. Her children were almost grown up and she really wanted to break out of the 'boring mum' mould before, as she put it, 'it was too late'. She had some savings that she had always thought might come in handy for the children, but decided to use them to achieve an ambition of her own – to learn to dive. The very thought of diving terrifies me, but I admired Catherine's determination as she proceeded to pass all her diving exams and a whole new (underwater) world opened up to her.

Emboldened by this, Catherine went on to fulfil other dreams that she had always nurtured but felt were out of her reach; she swam with dolphins in America and then spent three months backpacking around Europe, which she had never managed during her student years. As a result of these experiences, she blossomed into a totally new person. Her newfound confidence and happiness through her own personal achievements was wonderful to see and her children were thrilled at their newly adventurous mum.

Although you might want to shout your ambitions and intentions from the rooftops, be careful whom you share your plans and ideas with. If you are excited about something, avoid telling those people who, even with the best of intentions, may burst your bubble or even deliberately sabotage your excitement. We naturally want others to be as enthusiastic about our plans as we are, but it doesn't always work that way. The smallest negative comment from someone can 'burst the bubble' and leave us feeling deflated, disappointed and questioning our own enthusiasm. I'm not saying you should ignore valuable advice, particularly when it comes from someone whose opinion you respect, but you should protect yourself from those people who may wish to bring you down, for whatever reason.

TOP TIP: Other people may project their own fears on to you to try to stop you from doing something they would not wish to do themselves. Don't be put off by negativity from others if you really want to do something. Your time is your own and how you spend it should be your choice.

8
Sentimental value

Although I advocate a clutter-free existence, I must admit I am a sentimentalist at heart and therein lies the rub. How can you be both sentimental and clutter-free, when one involves the amassing of assorted ephemera and the other involves getting rid of it?

Sentiment is not a rational thing – it is seated in the heart and connects us with people and places we love and times we have enjoyed. There is nothing wrong with collecting items that remind you of such things, but many people fall into the trap of keeping too much stuff in the name of sentiment and then feeling overwhelmed by it.

When someone close to you dies, such as a parent, you may be the one who is left to sort out his or her possessions. I often work with bereaved individuals and I believe that everyone has a different 'right time' to get rid of things after a death. Some people find it easier to get rid of everything quickly, and may even be under pressure to do so if there is a house to be sold; for others it is a longer, more gradual process. Go at your own pace but, whatever you do, don't just leave it. Being surrounded by the belongings of another person, and perhaps the sad memories attached to them, is not good for your energy levels and will drag you down if left for too long. There is a time to grieve, but also a time to move on and continue your own life.

Death of a parent

I have found that one of the hardest tasks that people have to deal with is disposing of the effects of their parents. Even the smallest and most mundane items can move you to tears; a biscuit tin that you remember from childhood, a battered old tea cosy or a pair of spectacles; all can have special associations and will take on huge significance – they are your lasting physical reminders of a person who has been in your life longer than anyone else.

Helping clients to sort through the personal effects of a deceased relative is always a poignant exercise for me. The minutiae of existence form a snapshot of a life and I quickly build up a picture of the deceased person and a real sense of their personality. Although a lot of the stuff might be intrinsically valueless, I am acutely aware that these were the items that made up a life, yet once they are dispersed from the home they become anonymous objects that no one wants.

You may feel that stripping your parents' home of its contents is like dismantling the person you loved, but try not to be overtaken by your heart. If you try to absorb all their belongings into your own home you will quickly reach clutter crisis and I would strongly advise against it. You will already be feeling low after your bereavement and will find it very hard to move on if you are constantly surrounded by inherited clutter and the mental baggage that comes with it. Inherited clutter will not make you feel good, and giving it room in your own house simply delays the moment that you have to deal with its disposal.

I always advise clients to keep a few key items as reminders of the person they loved and then let the rest go. If you have inherited furniture you don't like, give it to charity so it will benefit someone else, or put it in an auction and buy something that you really like with the money gained from the sale. Get pleasure from knowing that the items will find new homes with people who will enjoy using them again.

Death of a partner

Anne

I started to work with Anne six months after she had lost her husband, John. He had been ill for several years and she was devastated when he died. They had no children, so Anne was valiantly struggling to get organized on her own, despite acute bad health and bouts of deep depression. Although they had been happily married for 30 years, John had been married before and Anne told me that the memory of his first wife (who had died young) had always been a shadowy presence in their marriage. John had been a historian, as well as an avid reader and keen collector. He was also a meticulous hoarder and there were many boxes of stuff, labelled in great detail, which Anne needed help to sort through and dispose of after his death.

I visited her every month for over a year, and little by little we sorted John's stuff. The deeper we went into the cupboards, the older the stuff was that we pulled out. Being taller, I stood on the ladder and handed things down to Anne, who was sitting on a chair unpacking the boxes. Because of John's careful labelling, I knew what was in the boxes before I passed them to Anne and I was apprehensive when I found the box of love letters and photographs from John's early days with his first wife. It was a poignant and tender collection, a record of a young and passionate love, which included their marriage certificate, passports and his army ID badge. I could see at a glance that this relationship had been special and I understood why John had secretly preserved its memory and kept it from Anne.

Poor Anne. She felt very hurt and angry that John could have been 'so disloyal' to her by keeping these mementoes, but admitted to me that she felt a sense of relief to have found only these things, which were simply innocent keepsakes. 'I have reached the bottom of the barrel,' she said. 'There's nothing else to find out so now the only way for me is up.'

Anne did not wish to keep any of the photos or letters and she asked me if I could take them away and burn them for her, which I did. As I watched the photos melting into the flames, I felt a real sadness that the memory of this loving relationship had just disappeared, and although I had known neither of these people I felt strangely moved.

I continued to visit Anne. Some sessions she laughed at what we found, others she cried. For her, it was a long and rocky road through her grief and her clutter; it seemed like every time she got on to a straight run she would unexpectedly find something of John's – even a small item – that brought back all her feelings of grief again. At times she felt daunted by the amount of stuff she still had to deal with, but I kept urging her to look back at how far she had already come – and not forward at how far she still had to go.

Getting rid of things after a death

Rebuilding normality after you have lost a life partner or loved one is a long process. Getting rid of things that once belonged to that person is a huge step in acknowledging that they have gone. Some people feel that it is disrespectful or disloyal to get rid of things that belonged to a loved one, or that it in some way diminishes that person. This is not the case. If you love someone, whether they are here or not, they will always be important in your life, but you should not feel guilty about disposing of their belongings if you really don't wish to keep them. You don't need to be hardhearted about it, but turning your home into a shrine is not a healthy way forward for you.

If you are really struggling with getting rid of things, ask a close friend or relative to help you decide what could go first. You might find it easiest to get rid of stuff that you don't really like or that has no real sentimental attachment for you. Clothes are possibly the hardest things to part with as they are the most personal items, but some people want to get rid of clothes first.

There may be painful reminders everywhere in your home that you keep coming across when you least expect to. Designate a special place – perhaps a wardrobe or chest of drawers – where you can safely keep things that remind you of your loved one. I'm not suggesting that you strip your house entirely of daily reminders of someone, but that you make the memories manageable so you are not constantly overwhelmed as you try to get your own life back together.

People often ask me what they should do with collections, hobby equipment or valuable items that had belonged to their spouse, particularly when there are no children, or if the children have no interest in taking the items. An easy solution is to sell the items. Look in *Yellow Pages* for your local auction house, who will give you free valuations and sell items on your behalf. Or there may be local groups/associations whose members might like to buy certain items – your partner may well have been a member of one himself. One of my clients, whose late husband had been a keen stamp collector, was able to sell most of his stamp collection to other collectors in a local philately group and was happy to know that the stamps had gone to people who would appreciate them and look after them. Another solution is to donate items to places where they will be used and enjoyed by others who need them. One woman I worked with decided to donate all of her late husband's photo-graphic equipment to a sixth form college so that it could be used by 'A' level art students. Many people are happy to give things away if the items will be used and appreciated by others.

Photos

Whenever I give a public talk, irrespective of the age group I am speaking to, if I ask how many people have a big box of unsorted photographs at home, nearly every hand in the room goes up! If you have been stashing photos away for years, always meaning to sort them out but never quite getting round to it, start now. Don't wait until you have time because you never will. You have to *make* time. There is only one way to tackle years of photo neglect and, like any other de-cluttering task, that is bit by bit. There's no need to rush out and buy a dozen new photo albums – this just puts off the real task of dealing with the photos and only adds to your clutter.

Step 1

Dive into that photo box and pull out a few wallets of pictures. Go through each pack and throw away all the duffers: the ones that are out of focus, the ones that are of something that doesn't interest you or the ones that make you look fat! Aim to reduce each pack by at least a half. Don't be sentimental about bad pictures – even if they are of your children. What's the point of keeping bad ones?

Step 2

If you can remember vaguely when the photo was taken, write the date on the back. No need to annotate fully at this point or you'll make such slow progress you'll get bored and give up. Stand your sorted photos upright and in date order in an old shoebox (or similar) with something heavy behind them to stop them slipping down. If your photos are in batches, divide them up with an index card – for example, 'Family Holiday to France 2001'. Throw away the old photo wallets and negatives (you'll never need them, honestly!). Your aim is to consolidate all those miscellaneous wallets of photos into a nice chronological order.

Step 3

Large school photos or portraits will need their own folder or shallow box that they can lie flat in. These should also be dated.

Step 4

Once you have knocked your collection into shape, and radically reduced it, then you can treat yourself to new albums. Keep your albums in an accessible place so that you and your family can get them out when you want to enjoy looking at your photos.

There will be many reading this who have 'gone digital' and have all their pictures stored on their PC. Digital cameras are wonderful and give you the opportunity to edit at source and 'delete the duffers' immediately. It's fun seeing your holiday snaps as a slide show on the PC, but I hear many people say they miss having 'real photos' to show to others. There is something very appealing about the simplicity of opening up an album to view your pictures rather than turning on the computer.

Unwanted gifts

Like so many people, when my husband and I got married, we already had a house full of furniture and other items. Unlike my grandparents, who saved up for everything during their engagement, we weren't starting from scratch and didn't really need anything. Even so, many of our wedding guests were extremely generous and we did get some really beautiful presents. However, there were a number of gifts that could only be described as strange. There was the glass picture frame that for a long time I thought was an ashtray, and a set of ornaments that I suspect had been round the wedding gift circuit a few times already. We kept them for a respectable length of time, but then I discreetly got rid of them!

The question of what to do with unwanted gifts, whether they were for a wedding, anniversary, birthday or Christmas, is one that I am frequently asked. Obviously, nobody wants to appear ungrateful for gifts they've been given, but at the same time nobody wants to keep stuff they don't like.

Clients sometimes tell me they feel trapped by unwanted gifts. They feel guilty if they don't like the item, but dare not get rid of it in case the giver finds out. There may also be a sentimental element, if the gift reminds you of an occasion or person close to your heart. You probably feel you should like it, even if you don't, so the very thing that was supposed to give you pleasure is actually making you feel really uncomfortable!

My advice on this thorny issue is that you shouldn't feel obliged to keep unwanted gifts – just move them out of your life. If you really don't like something, pass it on to someone who does, change it, or give it to charity. It's unlikely that the giver will ever check to see if you still have their present, but if they do you simply need to have an excuse ready. 'It got broken' is always a good one for horrible ornaments or china; 'My niece loved it so much I gave it to her, hope you don't mind' works well for things like cuddly toys, clothes or jewellery, and 'It was so good I lent it to a friend' is perfect for things like CDs, books or DVDs.

There is perhaps one exception and that is gifts from children, who have memories like elephants and eyes like hawks! Just when you thought you'd got away with it, they will suddenly want to know where that special ornament is, so go carefully on this one. There is nothing wrong with retiring an ornament into a drawer for a while, as long as you can produce it when questioned!

Collections

Collecting can be great fun – there's nothing like the thrill of the chase and the satisfaction of acquiring a new piece. For some, a collection can be a lifetime interest, for others, it may be a passing fancy. My friend Katy used to be a keen collector of pigs (not real ones of course!), but what started as a manageable group on a shelf, quickly grew into a whole display case full of porcine pals. Pottery pigs, wooden pigs, wind-up pigs, cuddly pigs, doorstop pigs, tea-towel pigs – people bought new pigs for Katy on every possible occasion. After years of an ever-expanding collection, Katy just got bored with pigs! She put the word out for *'No more pigs!'* and eventually the collection drew to a close.

Like Katy, over the years, you may have grown out of whatever you have been collecting, or the collection might even have grown out of your home! Know *why* you are buying something and *where* it's going to go when you bring it home. I often work with clients who have been collecting for so many years they don't know what they have or even why they bought it in the first place.

Don't feel bad about getting rid of stuff, even if you have spent a lot of time and money acquiring it. There is a time for everything in your life. Acknowledge to yourself that you have moved on – sell your old collection, reduce it to a few favourite pieces, or give it away to someone who will love it as much as you once did.

Keeping correspondence

'Clutterbugs' are great sentimentalists at heart – an endearing quality, but one that I always find myself up against when I am trying to help them get organized. A trait that many clutterbugs share is that they save every single birthday card, letter, gift tag, etc. that they have ever received from those closest to them, all with memories attached. Sorting out so much sentimental stuff is an emotional process for most people and can't usually be done in a hurry. I would always advise people two things to stop them getting swamped by sentimental paperwork:

1 Don't attach too much sentimental value to paper.
2 Throw things away before they have a chance to turn into 'sentimental' items.

Caroline
Caroline came to me because she had a massive paper problem in her home office. Every inch of available space was filled with piles of paper. Cupboard doors stayed open because of bulging boxes of paper, and filing cabinet drawers couldn't be closed. Carrier bags were stacked on the floor, each containing a bundle of papers, and plastic crates contained yet more stuff. Caroline showed me a small set of files that she was using on a daily basis and admitted that she only accessed about 5 per cent of the papers in the rest of her office.

On closer inspection I discovered that almost all of these stored papers were at least 20 years old and related to a time in Caroline's life when she felt she had been at her peak – both professionally and personally. Old diaries and work papers jostled for space with 30-year-old bank statements and receipts, newspaper cuttings and theatre programmes. All of these essentially mundane items had, over the years, been imbued with a sentimental value and therefore became 'things to keep' – tangible reminders of times past. There were also boxes full of personal correspondence, birthday cards and love letters, collected over the years and never sorted out. Like an overgrown garden, sentimentalism can get out of hand if you don't keep an eye on it!

Caroline not only kept every item of correspondence ever sent

82

to her, but also the envelopes they came in. Although she was keen to reduce her paperwork, she believed it would be wrong to throw away any letters or cards from friends and family. She was adamant that every item sent to her with love should be kept.

If you are like Caroline, there will be nothing I can do to shake your belief, but I would urge you to examine your reasons for keeping things:

- Will you ever look at them again?
- Does re-reading old letters cause you happiness or pain?
- Would you be able to reduce your keepsakes by even half?
- Hanging on to too much sentimental clutter means you will have less space. How badly do you want to reclaim your space so that you can live in the here and now?
- Do you want your memories more than you want the space?
- If you got rid of the paper, would you still have the memories?

Like my client, there are many people who keep things to remind themselves of happy times in their past. But some people also keep things that remind them of sad times. Working closely with people I often find sad letters that brought them bad news, and these items can still produce tears and painful feelings. There is no point in hanging on to sadness and pain. Why do you want to remind yourself of how bad you once felt? Dispose of items that make you feel bad and you will be better able to move on.

TOP TIP: Don't bog yourself down in the past. The best memories will always be with you in your heart and your head. Sometimes looking back can make you regretful about the passing of time. Live for the moment. *Carpe diem.*

Memorabilia and souvenirs

Every year my daughter attends a big summer pop concert held in our local stadium. She always comes home with a bagful of promotional items that are given out. Posters, badges, whistles, T-shirts – all destined for the bedroom floor and thereafter the bin! They don't get kept for long because after the excitement of the event has passed they just look rather tacky – as do so many other souvenirs of big sporting or musical events.

Save your money when you go to a big event – resist buying silly hats, badges, souvenir programmes or flags. If you do succumb to these things, then be sensible about getting rid of them too. If you allow yourself to save all the stuff associated with all the big events you ever attend, you will soon be sinking in a souvenir swamp! The further away the event becomes, the less meaningful all the stuff becomes too. If you must, select a couple of souvenir items but get rid of the rest.

My husband, a great rugby fan, insists on keeping every programme and ticket from every Welsh rugby match he has ever attended. We lug these items around from house to house when we move and, to my knowledge, he has never looked at them, touched them or even knows where they are!

Some readers may say my husband's rugby programmes have a monetary value, and I agree some memorabilia for large sporting or musical events can sometimes become very collectible. However, to what lengths do you have to go to redeem that value, and is it worth the effort? How much of your space are you prepared to give up to something that may or may not eventually become valuable? How much is a clutter-free house worth to you?

School books

When I am helping clients to de-clutter I frequently come across whole collections of old school exercise books. I don't know why it is that people find these particular items so hard to throw away. I guess they encapsulate a happy time of our lives and have a certain naïve charm, but old exercise books can be remarkably similar. Why not select a couple of the best as amusing reminders and get rid of the rest?

Clothes

Clothes are a tangible reminder of the past. For me it's a beautiful evening gown that reminds me of my graduation ball; my father-in-law has his old Royal Marines uniform; and one of my friends still has her grandmother's wedding dress.

But too many old clothes will clog up your wardrobe, sap your energy and make you feel depressed. A few years ago I spent some time working with a woman who had five wardrobes full of clothes she no longer wore, all about twenty years out of date and two sizes too small for her. She had kept them because they reminded her of how slim she used to be and also because they had been expensive and hardly worn – too good to give away. In fact, this only served to make her feel bad every time she opened the wardrobe. One of the wardrobes was full of clothes that didn't even belong to her. They had been rescued from her grandmother's house after her death and were beautiful vintage items, but there were simply too many of them.

This woman had reached a point where she had so many old clothes that she had no room to keep her current ones. Although she had more clothes than I have ever seen under single ownership, she felt bogged down and depressed at never being able to find anything to wear and spent most of her time in a tracksuit!

Keeping a few sentimental items of clothing is quite acceptable, but beware of the shrinking wardrobe syndrome! When your sentimental clothes outnumber your current clothes, you need a serious wardrobe weed.

TOP TIP: There is always a good market for quality vintage clothing. Specialist dealers may be interested in some items, but eBay is the best place to display and sell any interesting vintage clothes or accessories that you wish to part with. (See Chapter 10.)

Past loves

I can't leave this chapter without blowing a kiss in the direction of past loves! I think everyone retains a secret corner of their heart for past loves, but leave them where they belong – in the past. Don't hang on to old love letters or photos from past, failed relationships.

TOP TIP: Live *and love* in the here and now.

9

Children: time for a cuddle

Love your children with your heart, not your wallet, goes the saying. I once read that all children would be a lot happier if their parents spent half the amount of money on them and twice the amount of time. Isn't it ironic that the whole process of trying to be a good parent involves spending time away from children while we are earning money to buy them things?

I know from my own experience that although kids *say* they want things, it's not always *things* that they really want. You don't necessarily need to buy them new stuff to keep them happy. They may be more satisfied with your undivided attention for an hour or two and a cuddle on the sofa. Yes, even teenagers still enjoy a cuddle from Mum, although they may not like to admit it! In our house we try hard to make time for family evenings when we turn off the television and get out the Monopoly set or some other family game. At other times I really enjoy sitting down with my children and making things: craft projects, cards or Christmas decorations. All children love it if you sit close and do things with them, instead of always running off to attend to other, 'more important', stuff.

Again, I do not speak from a pedestal. I know how hard it is to fit everything in, especially when you are a working parent, but time not spent with your children can never be bought back, no matter how much money you earn. Your children probably won't remember all the things you bought for them when they were growing up, but they will remember the things you *did* with them. Looking back at my own childhood, I know there wasn't much money, but I don't recall ever feeling deprived of anything.

If you feel guilty about not spending enough time with your children, don't compensate by buying them yet more things. Many parents see an extravagant shopping trip as a way of spending 'quality time' with their children. This simply cements the idea in children's heads that love is the amount of stuff your mum can afford to buy you and that you have to buy things in order to feel good. More new stuff will just add to your general household clutter and doesn't really compensate your children for time not spent with them. It also means you are perpetuating the cycle of earning more money = having less time + buying more stuff to compensate.

My daughter often tells me about her friends who have a steady supply of designer clothes and all the latest gadgets and gizmos. I tell her that love isn't equal to the amount your mum spends on you, but I still struggle between feeling irritated that these children are so over-indulged and guilty that I don't do the same for my child.

TOP TIP: For a happier family, do less *buying* with your children and more *being* with them.

Resist, resist, resist!

I've seen inside a lot of children's bedrooms during my years as a clutter doctor, and if I had a pound for every item of designer gear or expensive gadget that I had seen abandoned on the floor, my piggy bank would be full! Kids' desires are usually transient; they live for the moment and are easily diverted. When they are really desperate to have something, stand firm – if you hold out long enough, the moment will pass. Don't forget that manufacturers spend millions trying to seduce us into buying stuff. Children are especially prey to the marketing people, who rely on 'pester power' to make parents dig both deep and often into their pockets!

The 'must-have' console game

One Christmas, my daughter was desperate for a certain console game. Apparently all her school friends had it and it was an absolute 'must-have' on every teenage Christmas list, although personally I didn't feel it was a particularly suitable game for a child. Well, clever marketing kept demand high and had that game flying off the shelves in the shops. In some places there was even a waiting list for when new stocks arrived.

No knight searching for the Holy Grail could have looked harder than I did for this rarest of items, but I was always the mum who got to the shop the day after they had sold out. Not being quick enough off the mark, I never did manage to find the console game for her and knew that she was bitterly disappointed on Christmas Day when none of the shiny wrappings revealed the very item she had hoped for. Although she didn't go short of other gifts, I beat myself up for being a hopeless mother and retired to the kitchen to weep over the turkey, while my daughter retired to her bedroom, also in tears, to text her friends what an awful Christmas she was having.

So you can imagine my relief when, two weeks after Christmas, my daughter told me she was glad not to have received the game after all, as she had borrowed it from a friend and didn't like it much anyway!

Fran

When I met her, Fran was 39 and a full-time mother of three. She was feeling stressed and depressed.

She felt her home was completely out of control and the children's stuff was everywhere. She said they weren't helping to tidy things away and she was sick of living in a mess. On my first visit to her I discovered that she was quite right – there *were* toys all over the place; far more toys than three children could ever play with, and clothes too, piles of them everywhere. The children were at the best school that money could buy and their father worked long hours in order to fund the lifestyle that they had chosen.

Whenever I met the children they were always being bundled into the car to go to drama lessons, football, tennis club, horse-riding, etc. They didn't come home from school until early evening and never seemed to have time to play with all their toys. They were nice kids, but when I talked to them I realized that they didn't want half of what they had and felt as overwhelmed by it as their mum. They were in fact quite happy to let things go, but it was their mother who wanted to hang on to every last book, board game and pencil stub. Even scrunched-up bits of paper with childish notes on them had to be kept, 'in case the children missed them', along with tatty old hairbands and little plastic trinkets from Christmas crackers, broken wax crayons and fast food 'freebie' toys. All the general low-cost junk that floats around in children's bedrooms everywhere was closely examined by Mum, picked over and kept – 'just in case' the children wanted it.

After several visits to a client I usually get to know them quite well and they tell me all sorts of things about themselves. Fran told me that she had grown up in one of the poorest areas of Liverpool, her father had been out of work for long periods, and her own mother had struggled to make ends meet. Frugality and thrift had been a way of life for her for so long that even now, when she was living very comfortably, there was an inbuilt fear of letting things go. This fear, combined with a natural hoarding instinct, had resulted in a clutter catastrophe! Far more stuff flowed into Fran's house on a daily basis than left it, and as a family they were all suffering the effects of too many things.

The downstairs area of the house was spacious and seemed to withstand the excess clutter; however, upstairs was unbearable and totally claustrophobic. The landing had become a temporary library with bookcases full of old paperbacks standing against every wall and a holding bay for broken things that were waiting for Daddy to mend when he came home.

Unsuccessful attempts had been made to clear the clutter – there were plastic sacks of children's clothes waiting to go up into the loft and boxes of toys that had been moved out of the children's rooms, but had got no further. The youngest child had become the recipient of 'hand-me-down everything' from his two older siblings and so his room had become the place where all the old toys, books and clothes ended up. Poor child – powerless to stop the flow of stuff and unable to play tidily (what child can?), his mother was always nagging him to do something about his room, but in truth it was she who had made it so bad.

Although Fran was always worrying about the price of everything, I noticed that she had a big spending habit and could not curb herself, particularly with the children. They wanted for nothing; in fact, they were overloaded with stuff. They hadn't asked for most of it, but their mum got cross with them if they didn't play with it and said that they were ungrateful. Each child's bedroom was full, they had a playroom downstairs, also full, and a garage bulging with bikes and other outdoor toys. I felt that the children were being suffocated with stuff, both toys and clothes. Their mother spent excessive amounts of time and money shopping and was always struggling to keep the house tidy.

One day she asked me if I thought the children had too many things and I had to say 'yes'. She was surprised and a bit defensive.

I urged her to simplify their lives by reducing the stuff in the bedroom of each child by 50 per cent. That seems like a lot, but, believe me, these rooms were *bursting*! I knew that the children

89

wouldn't miss their stuff once it had gone and that they would be able to sleep better, work better and play better in rooms that allowed them space.

Fran herself would have more time if she had less stuff to tidy up and would feel more in control, instead of sinking under toys all the time. I helped her to organize a huge garage sale one weekend. The children were fantastic. They were able to let stuff go so easily and it showed their mum that they weren't too bothered about keeping most of it. They raised several hundred pounds that I persuaded Fran to divide up between the children and put in their savings accounts, instead of going out and buying more new stuff. The family now holds a garage sale three times a year and each child has a 'sale box' in the bottom of their wardrobe that they can add to whenever they come across items that they no longer want. (For more about garage sales and car boot sales, see Chapter 10.)

Treasured possessions

I don't consider myself a heartless mother, but in my experience children don't miss most of their things once they've gone. They are very fickle creatures and quickly move on to new and more interesting stuff if it's presented to them. However, there are, in most families, some important and genuinely treasured children's possessions that I would never for one minute suggest you should dispose of. I'm sure you would know instantly what these are if you were challenged to pick out your child's most loved toy. (See more on sentimental items in Chapter 8.) Ours was Peter Rabbit – *now* totally unrecognizable after many years' use, he is just a rather dirty, smelly old piece of raggy stuff, residing peacefully under my teenage daughter's pillow and only coming out in emotional emergencies. But as the most senior toy in our household, he is still held in high esteem and we would happily get rid of many other things before him!

I would suggest that if something hasn't been touched since last year (and you'll know this because of the thick layer of dust on it), you should get rid of it; your children probably won't even notice that it's gone. It's a fact that children enjoy their space more than their stuff, so *reduce* and *simplify* – have less stuff!

TOP TIP: If you are nervous about getting rid of children's stuff, pack it away for six months and see if your children ask for it. If they don't notice it's gone, and never mention it again, you are safe to take the whole box to charity.

Children and sentiment

A simple rule here is *not too much*!

If you have more than one child you will know that with the first you take photos assiduously, save locks of hair and first teeth in special little pots, fill in the baby book and take loads of camcorder footage. For the second and subsequent children, you are not exactly less enthusiastic, but you just run out of steam for preserving all the details. With a growing family to look after, daily survival becomes the top priority. Just getting through the day is enough, without having to fiddle about trying to preserve memories too!

Many people keep far too many old baby clothes and equipment simply because it's a last link with a time that's now passed. You might feel getting rid of clothes that your children wore is almost like throwing away a part of them. But the more stuff you stash away in the loft, the more you'll feel overwhelmed by it and eventually it will have to go.

My friend Joey had four children, all now grown up. Since they were babies she has moved several times, been divorced and has now re-married. Over the years she has let all of her baby stuff go and is now a grandmother herself so feels she has come full circle.

Many years ago, as their family babysitter, I felt very attached to her children and asked if I could keep baby William's first shoes. For 25 years I kept those little shoes, hidden away in my special memory box, and I was recently delighted to be able to return them to Joey. She was thrilled to have such a precious item returned to her after so long, particularly as she herself had kept very few reminders of when her own children were tiny. Finding the middle ground is hard. You can't save every single item associated with your children, but getting rid of the lot can make you regretful later.

TOP TIP: Set up a special keepsake box for each child so you can save carefully chosen items as they grow up. Their first sleepsuit, shoes, lock of hair, favourite toy or school tie. Treasure the past, but don't swamp yourself with memories and don't feel you *have to* save every single item that belonged to your child.

What should you keep?

Artwork and craft projects

Select the best and bin the rest. A box file or two for each child should be big enough to hold a good selection of their pictures and writing. Large craft models that they have made can be photographed. Keep the model on display for as long as you like, but eventually you will need to throw it away.

If your child is older, ask them which bits are their favourites and which they no longer want. They are very often the best judges. Remember to write your child's name and the date on the back of any pieces you keep – don't rely on memory.

Certificates and exam results

Set up a ring binder with plastic sleeves inside to store all your child's reports, certificates and exam results.

Frame it

Avoid messy, dog-eared and oversized pieces of paper stuck up on the fridge door or on the kitchen wall. Invest in some simple wooden frames and make a feature of your child's best pieces of work. Arrange four or six frames together for impact. Change the pieces frequently so the work is always current. Your child will love to see his/her work properly displayed and you won't have messy bits of paper everywhere and sticky stuff on the walls.

School papers

Chucking out old school stuff, whether at primary school level or after big exams like GCSEs and 'A' levels, is a great sign of moving on and a cathartic process for your children. It signals new beginnings and focuses them on what lies ahead. Throw out redundant old school books and papers at the end of every year before time turns them into sentimental items, after which it becomes harder to part with them. (See Chapter 8.)

TOP TIP: Don't be too sentimental about children's paperwork – remember that it's quality and not quantity that counts.

Children's clothes

In most of the family homes I visit the children have more clothes than the adults! There are three types of clothes:

1 Clothes in current use.
2 Clothes to grow into.
3 Clothes that have been grown out of.

Children's clothes can quickly turn into bedroom clutter, so keep them under constant review. Regularly cull unworn and outgrown clothes from cupboards and drawers. Throw away old underwear and worn-out socks, and pass items in good condition on to friends, charity shops, or sell at a car boot sale. Don't let piles of clothes build up on bedroom surfaces. If clothes are to be given away, bag them up and put them straight in the car; if they are for mending, mend them the next time you sit down to watch television; if you are saving them for a car boot sale, put them in a bin-bag, label it, and store it in the garage. If you don't get round to a car boot sale within six to eight weeks, take the bag to a charity shop. When you are saving clothes for the next child to grow into, set aside a drawer or box in their wardrobe for 'growing into' items. Twice a year, check to see which clothes can be brought into use.

Some mothers, who have bought designer clothes for their children, may feel the clothes were too expensive to just give away once they have been grown out of. If this is the case for you, you may wish to consider selling these, either through a local agency or on eBay (see pages 101–3).

Organize clothes drawers
Help children to stay tidy by organizing their clothes drawers. Divide drawers into:

- Socks and undies.
- Nightwear.
- Tops.
- Bottoms.
- School wear.

Use shoeboxes or small plastic baskets as drawer dividers – put in

93

two or three to keep socks, pants and swimwear separate. Label the outside of the drawers or, if you have very young children, stick a picture on to show what's in each one. This way even the youngest members of the family can help put away the clean clothes and know where to find things.

Make clothes last

Children often shoot up in length, while staying the same in breadth! If last year's jeans still fit around the waist, turn them into this year's shorts by cutting off the legs and fraying the hems.

You don't always have to buy more

Most children have far too many clothes, so save yourself money and don't buy them extra things if they don't really need them. Children find too much of anything overwhelming, and clothing is no exception.

If you buy new clothes for your children and they don't like them, return the items to the shop *immediately* and get a refund, don't leave it until it's too late.

Children and television

Like many parents, I am concerned about the total amount of time that my children spend in front of a screen – television or computer. In a study entitled 'Television and the Socialization of Young Children', Huston and Wright at the University of Kansas said that 'children spend more time watching television than in any other activity except sleep'. Research suggests that children aged between 11 and 15 spend an average of 53 hours a week (7.5 hours a day) watching television and computer screens, an increase of 40 per cent in the last decade, with about half of all children now having a television or computer in their bedrooms. Worrying statistics indeed.

Professor George Gerbner of the University of Pennsylvania carried out a study in the 1960s on the influence of television on the viewers' perception of the world. He believed that over a period of time television can have a gradual but cumulative effect on viewers that can significantly affect their attitude and beliefs rather than their behaviour. Gerbner called this 'cultivation theory'. His study focused on 'heavy viewers', who he said were more likely to be influenced by the ways in which the world is portrayed in television programmes than those who watched television less. This is especially the case for individuals who may have little first-hand experience of certain topics, and so rely on the television as their main source of information. In 1990 a similar study by Judith van Evra argued that younger viewers may depend on television for information more than other viewers, who might have access to other sources of information (van Evra, 1990, page 167).

Alternative activities

You are the one who has to provide a fun alternative to get your children away from the television or computer. Lots of kids are simply out of the habit of entertaining themselves, but it's not difficult to get them interested in other things.

Board games don't have to be *bored* games! Get out the Monopoly, Cluedo or even a pack of cards; sit down and do something 'crafty' with your children, or take them outside for a game of football; don't let them think they are being deprived by not watching television.

Use the library

Don't forget that your local library is still a fantastic free source of information and entertainment. If you haven't been there for a while, why not make a special trip to check it out? Make a note in your diary of the return date for your library books, DVDs or other borrowed items. Save money by reading magazines and newspapers in the library instead of buying them.

Special occasions

It's hard to enjoy special occasions in a simple way. The marketing men seize every opportunity to make us, the punters, buy more useless stuff in order to feel we are 'doing' an occasion properly.

Valentine's Day, Mothering Sunday, Father's Day, Easter, Halloween, Thanksgiving, Christmas, and of course birthdays and anniversaries. All year long there is some excuse for us to go out and spend money on cards and gifts. You will probably feel under immense pressure to go along with some, if not all, of this. Not doing so may make you fear you appear churlish and a bit of a misery.

Make a conscious effort to turn away from 'commercialism' and celebrate these occasions in a family way so that your children feel you are not being a complete 'party-pooper'. Suggest that you make cards for each other instead of buying them, and have a very small budget for gifts, even placing a veto on shop-bought gifts for occasions like Valentine's Day, Mothering Sunday, Easter, etc. You don't need to bring more stuff into your home to prove that you love each other – time spent together is far more valuable and your children will remember it longer than yet another shop-bought gift.

Celebration tea

A good old-fashioned 'tea party' is a great and simple way to bring the family together. Even though my children are older now, they still love this type of party, with jelly and ice-cream, fairy cakes, sandwiches, sausages on sticks, etc. Whatever the age of your children, they will love the sense of occasion that a 'celebration tea' brings and the excitement of getting ready for it. Have a colour-themed table, make decorations and place cards, use a matching cloth and candles. Design a special menu and put a fun spin on ordinary food by giving things fancy names. Dress up, use the best china, and place a small gift by everyone's plate. Resist buying anything extra. Be inventive, improvise with what you already have.

TOP TIP: If you want to keep things simple, the power is in your hands. Resist commercialism and focus on family. Have home-made things where possible and set budgets for occasions where overspending is likely – such as at Christmas.

Empty-nesters

I can't leave this chapter on children without mentioning grown-up children who leave their clutter at home for their parents to look after! If you are an 'empty-nester', acting as a clutter caretaker for your adult children, you are in a difficult situation. So many adult children use their parents' home as a free storage facility. How many bedrooms where the occupant has long since gone are still cluttered up with items that were not important enough to be taken away by the owner?

If you are harbouring stuff for your grown-up 'child', and *especially* if they now have their own home, tell them you are going to box up their remaining possessions and they have to collect them by a certain date, after which you'll give them to charity. You are not rejecting your child by doing this, just reclaiming your space! Be tough – you are not a storage facility!

Rules for clutter caretakers

- Be careful about what you agree to store.
- Set a time limit on how long you keep things for.
- Agree what will happen to items when the time is up.
- Don't let others make you responsible for deciding what happens to the stuff.
- Avoid storing big things like furniture, old cars, bikes, etc.

Finally . . .

Remember that you, as a parent, can have a direct influence on your children's future spending habits. Teach them how to spend wisely, how to live simply, and how *being* can be just as enjoyable as *buying*. Make our future generations less wasteful and more satisfied with less stuff. Happiness can't be brought home in a carrier bag.

10
Staying organized

Sometimes when I start work with a client they think that a few visits from me, along with a liberal sprinkling of fairy-dust, will get them organized once and for all and they will stay that way for ever. Well, I can definitely help them get organized, but I'm afraid there is no 'organizational nirvana'. Being organized is not an ultimate state that you achieve and then magically stay that way. Life isn't like that. Just as maintaining weight loss requires healthier eating habits, so maintaining an organized space requires better organizational habits. Both these things mean you have to take a different approach to your life, and yes – be more disciplined with yourself!

There is bound to be some slippage at busy times. Too many things going on at once always impact on the state of your home – and mind! Don't be hard on yourself. 'I've tried being organized and it doesn't work' is a phrase I often hear. *Nobody is perfect!* Don't give up and surrender to your clutter again. Make small changes to keep yourself better organized, and if you feel you can't manage it on your own, make a regular booking every few months with a professional organizer who can get you back on track.

Here are a few checkpoints to bear in mind:

Devise an 'Anti-Shopping' List

If you are disorganized, there's a strong chance that you buy too much stuff simply because you can't find the things you have already bought, so you have to keep buying more. Cure the over-buying habit and you are halfway to curing the clutter habit (and saving a whole load of money!).

When I am working with people, I often discover stashes of things that they have bought, hidden away to use later, and then forgotten about. For one person, it was black tights, for another, it was envelopes, for another it was notebooks. They are delighted when they find these hidden supplies in various places throughout the house, but it usually means they have far more than they need. When this is the case, I write out an Anti-Shopping List for them to remind them what *not* to buy!

Over-buying is often the result of a fear that you are going to run out. Running out of stuff is not a life and death issue – it's just a nuisance, but you can live with it. Don't clog your cupboards with too many 'just in case' supplies. Leave them in the shops until you need them.

Get rid of store cards

The only real beneficiary of you signing up for a store card is the store – no matter how well they sell it to you. *Just say no!*

Make do and mend

I'm not suggesting that you go to some of the extremes of wartime thrift, but this favourite wartime slogan can be adapted for life today. Think carefully about replacing goods that are still usable, just because you are fed up with them. Make your furniture and household stuff go on that bit longer, mend your clothes instead of getting rid of them, use up food instead of throwing it away, use the central heating less, and walk instead of using the car.

Keep giving stuff away

Have a permanent charity box or carrier bag for whenever you come across something you no longer use or love. When it's full, don't look in it – take it straight to a charity shop or supermarket recycling point.

Bin the breakages

If something gets broken and is not easily repairable, bin it immediately. Don't put it on the window sill or shove it in the garage to deal with 'later' – later never comes.

Outgoing items

Have a basket, box or bag near your front door for 'outgoing items' such as letters to post, library books to be returned, clothes for dry cleaning. When you are going out, just pick up the whole thing and put it in the car with you. (Note: Unless they're too heavy, post items to people – don't save things for months until you see the person. You'll feel great to have got things off your plate at last – one more bit of clutter leaving the house.)

Throw away every day

Excessive paper is the single most common cause of disorder in people's homes today. Don't let paper overwhelm you. Throw some away every day. Growing paper piles are a dangerous sign and should never be left unattended! Don't put aside stuff 'to look at later' – we know that 'later' will probably never come. And don't allow yourself the luxury of dithering over whether you might want certain newspaper cuttings or torn-out recipes – just throw them away! More will appear.

Gifts

Shopping for gifts can be the most soul-destroying and time-wasting activity. Shop online – buy a good book at Amazon or take a look at some of the charity gift websites. For weddings, stay safe; stick to the list or simply give money/vouchers. For birthdays and Christmas, unless the recipient has indicated a particular item that they want, again save yourself time and effort with a gift voucher. If you want to turn up with something more than just an envelope, add a good box of chocolates, some quality bath stuff or a beautiful bouquet of flowers.

A present box is great for last minute invitations to children's parties, teachers' gifts, etc. – but don't overbuy for it.

Use stuff up

Every year we have a thrift month in our home – it's usually January – when we challenge ourselves to spend the smallest amount of money we can, and use up supplies that we already have in the house. I try to use up all the food that's in the freezer and store cupboard, and my husband and I stop drinking alcohol for the month. We work our way through all the gift toiletries and stationery from Christmas and anything we don't want goes into our present box so we can use it as a gift for someone else. I enlist the help of the children; we call it 'The Skinflint Challenge' and they love it. It feels good to give yourself permission to stop spending and also to feel that the level of stuff in your home is reducing.

What shall I do with it?

I know that most people would prefer their stuff to go to someone who will make good use of it, but finding a disposal route for your things requires both time and effort. However, don't make this an excuse not to de-clutter. There are plenty of ways to dispose of your unwanted items.

Selling is a great way to turn clutter into cash, but – a note of caution. I know several people who never get rid of anything that they think they can sell. Fair enough – there's nothing wrong with selling things. The problem is that they never get round to doing it. If you don't have time for the process of selling, or you're not thrilled at the thought of standing at a car boot sale for hours, then it's *far better* to give your stuff away to charity. You're not losing money, you're saving time and making your life simpler by getting rid of stuff, at the same time as benefiting a charitable cause.

Charity shops

These should be your first port of call, particularly for smaller items. Most charity shops take clothes, jewellery, books, toys, tapes/CDs and household goods. Make sure all your donations are in good, saleable condition: broken or incomplete items have to be thrown away. (Oxfam says it spends £1 million every year simply getting rid of unsaleable items.) Due to safety legislation, charity shops will no longer take electrical goods and some shops have rules about accepting baby equipment like prams, high chairs, etc. A quick phone call before loading up the car is always a good idea if you are in any doubt. Some charities have now set up specialist bookshops and music shops. If donated items, such as rare or old books/records, have a collectable value, they are priced accordingly by specialists, so you know that your donations are raising the highest amount of money for the charity.

Car boot sales

Spend a Sunday morning turning your clutter into cash. This is a great way to get rid of your stuff quickly, but only if you keep your prices low. Remember that people go to car boot sales to pick up

101

bargains. If you price high, then you won't sell – remember the aim is to get rid of your stuff. A £2 coin in your pocket is better than an unused item taking up cupboard space in your home. Don't price something based on what you paid for it when it was new – this is of no interest to your average buyer at a car boot sale.

Must-have equipment for a car boot sale
- A wallpapering table or a plastic garden table to display your goods.
- A float of loose change, kept in a waistbag, not on the table.
- A rail to hang clothes on.
- A supply of carrier bags.
- Plastic sheeting to spread on the ground for displaying extra items.

Beware the 'early birds' who will want to pick through your boxes even before you have unloaded them from the car. These are usually the dealers who cream the best stuff off all the stalls first thing. Don't let them browbeat you into lowering your prices too early.

Charity sales
Charity sales such as church fêtes or school fairs may offer the chance to hire a stall and sell your things on behalf of your favourite charity. Bric-à-brac, gift items, books and good-quality housewares always sell well at these sorts of events. Make sure that everything is clean, in good condition and clearly priced.

Garage sales
These are a good way of selling larger items such as garden or household furniture. Make sure you have plenty of family members or friends to help you. Advertise your sale in your local paper, newsagent's window, and on a board outside your house. Don't forget to warn your neighbours, as your garage sale will bring more cars than usual into your road.

Auctions
Many specialist auction houses deal in antiques and top-quality valuables, and you can often obtain free valuations. More general auctions sell collectible and household goods. If you've never been to an auction, but would like to try selling your stuff this way, I suggest you go along to one first to see how the process works. They

are great fun and many auctioneers are real showmen, guaranteeing an entertaining few hours. Try to resist the temptation to buy anything – remember you are aiming to reduce your clutter, not acquire more!

eBay

The world's biggest virtual auction, you can buy and sell just about anything on eBay, but if you don't have time or it seems too complicated, contact a local eBay Registered Trading Assistant, who, for a percentage fee, will sell your stuff for you – completely hassle free! To find a Trading Assistant in your area go to <www.ebay.co.uk>, click on 'Advanced Search' at the top right-hand corner of the home page, and then click on 'Find a Trading Assistant'.

Freecycle

If you're feeling altruistic and would rather give your stuff away than sell it or chuck it, visit <www.freecycle.org>. Advertise your unwanted items and they can be collected free of charge by anyone who is interested in them. The Freecycle rule is that no money exchanges hands and the principle is that items are 'free to a good home'.

Recycling

Look on the very excellent <www.recyclenow.com> website for all sorts of useful recycling ideas, tips and addresses. So much of what we throw away can now be recycled – there's no excuse not to!

Particular items – what shall I do with them?

Old tools

Donate them to the Christian charities 'Tools With a Mission' (TWAM) or 'Tools for Self Reliance' (TFSR), both of which collect and recondition hand tools and send them to Africa and other poorer countries to help people become self-sufficient (<www.TWAM.co.uk> or <www.tfsr.org>).

Mobile phones

Some phones, in good working order and with the charger, can be worth as much as £5 to a charity. Don't just give your old phone to the kids to play with – donate it!

Printer cartridges

Again, many charities want your empty printer cartridges to recycle, so don't chuck them out.

Paint

Nearly everyone has unused tins of paint in their garage or shed. Contact <www.communityrepaint.org.uk>. Community Repaint is a network of paint re-use schemes across the UK.

Furniture

There are many charities in the UK who will take good-quality, secondhand furniture, provided it meets the Furniture and Furnishings Safety Regulations 1988. Contact your local council for details of charities near you who collect unwanted furniture.

Computers

Computer recycling schemes are on the increase; some schemes recondition machines to be sent to poorer countries, others offer environmentally safe disposal. The website <www.envocare.co.uk/computers.htm> lists a variety of schemes and contacts to help you dispose of your computer ecologically.

Bicycles

The website <www.re-cycle.org> collects and ships secondhand bicycles and parts to Africa, where they provide much needed transport.

Spectacles

Ask your optician if he or she collects old spectacles for charity recycling, or contact the 'World in Sight' appeal run by Help the Aged, which collects and sends spectacles to developing countries. (See Useful addresses at the back of this book.)

Living with other people's clutter

I'm often contacted by people who say they want to help a friend or relative who is chronically cluttered. When the enquiry is from a third party like this, there is unfortunately not a great deal of practical help I can give. Some people are quite happy living in a cluttered state and don't want to be helped out of it. No matter how bad it may appear to you, if this is their chosen way of living, then you have to let them get on with it.

However, if you are unfortunate enough to be sharing your home with a clutterbug, and they are imposing their mess on you, then that's quite a different thing. You have a right to feel comfortable in your own space and should not have to put up with someone else's mess. I have seen many relationships foundering on the rocks of extreme clutter, and I can't stress how important it is not to impose your clutter on the one you love. If you love and respect someone, you should also love and respect their space. There is no reason why they should have to suffer your clutter.

Talk to your partner and tell them how their clutter makes you feel. Ask if you can work together to clear some space, or if they would agree to seek professional help. Your partner will probably be, in turn, defensive and upset, but if you don't do anything, the problem will get worse. Let your partner know that you want to help and not criticize, and that you will give him or her every support to overcome the problem.

Marcus and Louisa

Marcus phoned me about his wife Louisa and her obsessive clutter habit, which had reached a critical point. I was relieved when Louisa agreed to speak to me directly as it meant she was in agreement to my helping her. She told me that she was finding it hard to deal with the backlog of stuff she had accumulated since they had moved into their new house, especially as she had little time and two very young children to look after. She said she was not essentially an untidy person, but had a real problem getting rid of things as she thought she might need them again.

I arranged to visit them – and I must admit that I too felt overwhelmed by the amount of stuff they had everywhere! I didn't know how they were functioning as a family, and felt that Marcus had called me in as a last attempt at rescuing them from sinking, both emotionally and physically, under the clutter. Although the house was a good size, there was nowhere to sit and eat, relax or even walk around, and the kitchen was only just functioning. The children were fractious and badly behaved and I sensed that they too were suffering from the chaotic lifestyle brought about by excess everything.

I helped Louisa to identify the key area that would make the most difference to them as a family. This was the dining room, where the table was buried under miscellaneous rubbish, the ironing pile nearly reached the ceiling, and children's toys lay all over the floor. Louisa was very nervous of me touching anything at all, but got braver as the day wore on. I asked her permission before I threw anything away, and although this made progress extremely slow, it allowed a level of trust to build up between us. Marcus was the most supportive husband I had ever met and stayed by Louisa all day, encouraging her when she wavered, bringing us regular tea and biscuits when we started to flag, and loading the car with rubbish to dispose of as we bagged it up. Louisa told me she was seeking counselling for her obsessive hoarding, and both she and Marcus spoke freely about her compulsion. I am telling you this to illustrate that a serious hoarding problem *can* be addressed in a supportive and non-threatening way, but there has to be love and understanding and a willingness to make changes.

I was delighted at the end of the day to have been able to restore the dining room to a fully functioning space and I knew that Louisa was really proud of herself for having faced her problem head on. Later on that evening, when I got home, I received an e-mail from her and Marcus saying they had just enjoyed their first family meal sitting round their dining table for about six months. The children had been thrilled to sit down properly with Mummy and Daddy and the orderly space was reflected by much calmer behaviour from them. Both Marcus and Louisa said they were looking forward to making further positive changes in their life.

Conclusion

We all know our own limits, but sometimes we are very bad at recognizing when we have reached them. If you have successfully cut back on your spending and reduced your commitments so that your finances and time are both more manageable, *keep it like that*! Don't spoil your efforts by allowing extra spending or extra commitments to creep back in, just because you can. You already know that inviting extra things into your life has a knock-on effect on everything else. Be strict with yourself – say 'no' and stay balanced.

Some final 'Do's' and 'Don'ts'

- Don't set up over-complicated systems for yourself.
- Don't take on too many extra commitments.
- Don't buy too much.
- Don't say yes too often.
- Don't be scared to get rid of things.

- Do give things away freely.
- Do have places for everything.
- Do know your own threshold.
- Do spend *time* on yourself, not money.
- Do love others with your heart, not your wallet.

Having helped so many people to reduce their possessions and reorganize their lives, I know that my golden rule of 'Reduce and Simplify' really works. Simplifying your life and staying organized need not be a chore, and it's not about depriving yourself. It's just about putting the brakes on your spending, reducing what you own, and simplifying the way you do things.

Don't waste your time and resources acquiring things you don't need. Time spent reducing your stuff now will give you more time to spend on yourself, and with those you love, in years to come.

Useful addresses

De-cluttering and organizers

Association of Professional Declutterers and Organisers UK
Website: www.apdo-uk.co.uk

Clearly Organised
Professional de–cluttering and organizing service run by Naomi Saunders
Tel.: 07799 126 195
Website: www.clearlyorganised.co.uk

Professional Organizers Web Ring (USA)
Website: www.organizerswebring.com

For help if you have had a bereavement

Cruse Bereavement Care
Cruse House
126 Sheen Road
Richmond
Surrey TW9 1UR
Tel.: 020 8940 4818
Bereavement helpline: 020 8332 7227
To speak to a counsellor in afternoons or evenings, phone 0345 585 565
Website: www.crusebereavementcare.org.uk

Cruse also offers a large range of books: see website for details.

War Widows Association of Great Britain
c/o 48 Pall Mall
London SW1 5JY
Tel.: 0870 2411305
Website: www.warwidowsassociation.org.uk
E-mail: info@warwidowsassociation.org.uk

Bereavement Register

This aims to supply names of the recently deceased to mail order companies to ensure that names and addresses are removed from their databases. To register details, phone 0870 600 7222.

Deceased Preference Service

This is a similar scheme to the Bereavement Register. Visit www.deceasedpreferenceservice.co.uk for more details and an online registration form.

For general information on death and dying

www.ifishoulddie.co.uk

For help if you are in debt

Credit Action
Howard House
The Point
Weaver Road
Lincoln LN6 3QN
Tel.: 01522 699777
Website: www.creditaction.org.uk
E-mail: office@creditaction.org.uk

Consumer Credit Counselling Service (CCCS)
Wade House
Merrion Centre
Leeds LS2 8NG
Tel.: 0800 138 1111 (Freephone helpline open 8 am to 8 pm Monday to Friday)
Website: www.cccs.co.uk
E-mail: contactus@cccs.co.uk

For help with phobias, anxiety and other emotional difficulties

In the UK

British Association for Counselling and Psychotherapy
35–37 Albert Street
Rugby
Warwickshire CV21 2SG
Tel.: 0870 443 5252 (8.45 am to 5 pm, Monday to Friday)
Website: www.bacp.org.uk
E-mail: bacp@bacp.org.uk

USEFUL ADDRESSES

Details of counselling organizations and services in your local area.

Depression Alliance
212 Spitfire Studios
63–71 Collier Street
London N1 9BE
Tel.: 0845 123 2320
Website: www.depressionalliance.org
E-mail: information@depressionalliance.org

National Phobics Society
Zion Community Resource Centre
339 Stretford Road
Hulme
Manchester M15 4ZY
Tel.: 0870 122 2325
Website: www.phobics-society.org.uk
E-mail: info@phobics-society.org.uk

No Panic
93 Brands Farm Way
Telford
Shropshire TF3 2JQ
Freephone helpline 0808 808 0545 (10 am to 10 pm, 365 days a year)
Website: www.nopanic.org.uk
E-mail: ceo@nopanic.org.uk

Seasonal Affective Disorder (SAD)
SAD Association
PO Box 989
Steyning BN44 3HG
Website: www.sada.org.uk

Sleep difficulties
Website: www.sleepnet.com

Devoted to improving sleep health worldwide.

In the USA

Anxiety Disorders Association of America
8730 Georgia Avenue, Suite 600
Silver Spring
MD 20910, USA
Tel.: (240) 485-1001
Website: www.adaa.org

For information on living more simply and slowly

Enough: Anti-Consumerism Campaign
Website: www.enough.org.uk

Inspirational Quotes
Website: www.stresslesscountry.com

Quotes that cover many different subjects that can help in the journey towards simpler living.

The Simple Living Network
Websites: www.simpleliving.net
www.simpleliving.net/seedsofsimplicity

Slow Food
Website: www.slowfood.com

An international organization whose aim is to protect the pleasures of the table from the threats posed by the fast-food culture and lifestyle.

For information on rest and spiritual refreshment

The Findhorn Foundation
The Park
Forres
Scotland IV36 3TZ
Tel.: 01309 690311
Website: www.findhorn.org
E-mail: enquiries@findhorn.org

The Retreat Association
The Central Hall
256 Bermondsey Street
London SE1 3UH
Tel.: 0845 456 1429
Website: www.retreats.org.uk
E-mail: info@retreats.org.uk

Publishes a brochure on retreat centres each year, available either through e-mail or at most Christian bookshops in the UK.

Recycling information

Composting

The Composting Association
Avon House
Tithe Barn Road
Wellingborough
Northants NN8 1DH
Tel.: 0870 160 3270 (general enquiries only; this is a membership organization)
Website: www.compost.org.uk

Garden Organic (the working name of the Henry Doubleday Research Association)
Ryton Organic Gardens
Coventry CV8 3LG
Tel.: 024 7630 3517 (general enquiries only; membership organization)
Website: www.gardenorganic.org.uk
E-mail: enquiry@hdra.org.uk

General recycling details

recycle-more
Valpak Ltd
Stratford Business Park
Banbury Road
Stratford-upon-Avon
CV37 7GW
Tel.: 08450 682 572
Website: www.recycle-more.co.uk
E-mail: recycle-more@valpak.co.uk

Recycling mobile phones

Oxfam Bring Bring Scheme
Freepost LON16281
London WC1N 3BR
(If you are donating more than ten phones, call 0870 752 0999.)
Website: www.oxfam.org.uk/what_you_can_do/recycle/phones/htm

Recycling printer cartridges

www.cartridges4charity.co.uk

www.recyclingappeal.com
Tel.: 08451 3020 10
E-mail: info@recyclingappeal.com

Runs recycling campaigns for many different UK charities. Takes printer cartridges, phones and Personal Digital Assistants, for example Palmpilots and Blackberries.

Recycling spectacles

Vision Aid Overseas
12 The Bell Centre
Newton Road
Manor Royal
Crawley RH10 9FZ
Tel.: 01293 535016
Website: www.vao.org.uk

World in Sight Appeal
c/o Help the Aged
207–221 Pentonville Road
London N1 9UZ
Tel. (recycling hotline): 0870 7700 446 (In Northern Ireland, call 02890 230 666)

Further reading

Belbin, David, *The eBay Book: Essential tips for buying and selling on eBay.co.uk*. Petersfield: Harriman House Publishing, 2004.

Belk, Russell, *Collecting in a Consumer Society*. London and New York: Routledge, 1995.

Evra, Judith van, *Television and Child Development*. New Jersey: Lawrence Erlbaum, 1990.

Fletcher, Ben; Pine, Karen; Penman, Danny, *The No Diet Diet: Do Something Different*. London: Orion, 2005.

Gladwell, Malcolm, *The Tipping Point: How Little Things Can Make a Big Difference*. London: Abacus, 2002.

Hall, Alvin, *What Not To Spend*. London: Hodder & Stoughton, 2004.

Hay, Louise L., *You Can Heal Your Life*. Carlsbad, Calif.: Hay House, 2002.

Holden, Robert, *Happiness Now!* London: Coronet Books, 1998.

Honoré, Carl, *In Praise of Slowness: How a Worldwide Movement Is Challenging the Cult of Speed*. New York: HarperCollins, 2004.

Lewis, Martin, *The Money Diet*. London: Vermilion, 2004.

McGee, Paul, *S.U.M.O. (Shut Up, Move On): The Straight-Talking Guide to Creating and Enjoying a Brilliant Life*. Oxford: Capstone Publishing, 2005.

Myers, David G., *The Pursuit of Happiness*. New York: Avon Books, 1993.

Nutt, David J., *Generalized Anxiety Disorder: Diagnosis, Treatment and Its Relationship to Other Anxiety Disorders*. Taylor & Francis, 2001.

Richardson, Cheryl, *Take Time for Your Life: A Seven-Step Programme for Creating the Life You Want*. London: Bantam Books, 1998.

Spicer, Lorne, *Find a Fortune: How to Buy, Sell and Make Money on EBay and at Boot Sales*. London: Orion, 2005.

Whybrow, Peter C., *American Mania: When More Is Not Enough*. New York: W. W. Norton & Company, Inc., 2005.

Index

activities: children's 94–5; cutting down 29; exercise 19; gyms and health clubs 53–4
Alabama, University of 6
alcohol and drugs 6
American Mania: When More Is Not Enough (Whybrow) 2
Amish communities 7–8
auctions 102–3

car boot sales 101–2
Celente, Gerald 1–2
charities 39, 101; ongoing giving 49, 99; school/church sales 102; types of donations 103–4; unused bargains from 55
children: activities 94–5; clothes 93–4; clutter left behind 96–7; healthy babies 7; keepsakes 91–2; special occasions 95–6; time and affection 86–7
chronic fatigue syndrome 19
clothes 84–5; after a death 78, 85; children's 93–4; make do and mend 99
clutter: disposing conscientiously 38–40; effects of 5–6; keeping/ letting go 39, 41; other people's 104–6; transition period 40–1; useful items for 35–7
Cognitive Behaviour Therapy (CBT): 'remoralization' 17
collections/hobbies 78, 81; memorabilia and souvenirs 83–4
computers: children and 94–5; internet time 64; recycling and donating 104
consumerism 2, 7; children and 57–8, 87–90; compulsive buying 15–17; pressure for 11–12; special occasions 95–6

Dement, Dr William 19

eBay 103
emotions and mental health factors: anxiety 7, 67; compulsiveness 15–17, 20; concentration 7; death of loved ones 75–8; depression 5, 17–18; guilt feelings 29; irritability 6; rewarding yourself 21; SAD 19; sentimental value 75–85
entertainment 56
Evra, Judith van 95

finances: borrowing cash 61; budgeting 58–9; buying unnecessarily 52–6; children and 56–8; store cards 99; track your spending 59
food: bulk buying 54; eating out 54; slow food movement 3; stress signs and 6; supermarkets 54; warehouse shopping 54

gardens 49
Gerbner, George 94
gifts: shopping for 100; unwanted 80–1

Hay, Louise 15
hoarding 31, 104–6
household administration: diaries, lists and notices 44–7; house meetings 45; make do, mend and bin 99; paperwork and post 42–4; receipts 59–60; shredding 47–8
household chores 66–7; help with 68, 71–2; laundry and cleaning 50–1; ten-minute tidy 72
Howard, Kenneth I. 17
Huston and Wright: 'Television and